HONEST
ANSWERS

HONEST ANSWERS

Interviewing and Negotiation Skills to Get to the Truth

LENA SISCO

HarperCollins
Leadership

An Imprint of HarperCollins

Published by HarperCollins Leadership, an imprint of HarperCollins Focus LLC.

Any internet addresses, phone numbers, or company or product information printed in this book are offered as a resource and are not intended in any way to be or to imply an endorsement by HarperCollins Leadership, nor does HarperCollins Leadership vouch for the existence, content, or services of these sites, phone numbers, companies, or products beyond the life of this book.

ISBN 978-1-4002-2642-9 (eBook)
ISBN 978-1-4002-2640-5 (TP)

Library of Congress Control Number: 2022940853

Printed in the United States of America
22 23 24 25 26 LSC 10 9 8 7 6 5 4 3 2 1

I am dedicating this book to my husband and best friend, who

offered me sound guidance. Thank you for your patience,

support, motivation, and wisdom. You are a great leader.

CONTENTS

CONTENTS

FOREWORD

by Janine Driver

• • •

"This should be a textbook for every criminal justice course, for every law enforcement agency, and for every HR department."

—JANINE DRIVER, CEO and founder of the Body Language Institute and *New York Times* bestselling author

On October 28, 2013, had you been in a chilly, small hotel room in Alexandria, Virginia, along with seven other classmates getting certified in detecting deception, perhaps you would have noticed what I noticed about Lena Sisco when she walked into the room . . .

Lena was personable, polished, professional, poised, and a dead ringer for Jennifer Aniston—except with a Rhode Island accent. Because I'm originally from Boston, I picked up on Lena's accent right away.

There was something about Lena, beyond the fact that we both used the word "wicked" to describe how awesome something was, that made me feel like she was a friend from high school or college whom I hadn't seen in years. In under a couple of minutes, I found Lena, this complete stranger to me, to be warmhearted, grounded, and wise.

Has this ever happened to you?

x

You're traveling in a different part of the country—or the world. Maybe you're in a workshop, on vacation, or at a coffee shop chatting with someone who likes the same kind of latte, and you suddenly have an instant rapport with this new kindred spirit.

Perhaps, like me, you can't explain it, but without realizing it, you let your guard down and you *trust*ed this new acquaintance because something inside of you told you *she's a friend* and you're *safe*. Soon, you're sharing with your "new friend" things you don't normally share with neighbors or co-workers, let alone a complete stranger!

How is this possible? And why did I connect with Lena right away?

I didn't read a bio about Lena Sisco. We weren't Facebook or Instagram friends. No one I knew vouched for the quality of Lena's character. Yet, within minutes, I felt that this stranger would become a friend for life.

I didn't know it then, but Lena had already unlocked what is behind those disarming moments when our walls come down—and she's sharing that knowledge in this book.

- Imagine what would be possible if you were able to have a step-by-step process to channel your ability to build an ultimate level of *rapport* and *trust*—at will.
- Imagine the impact you'd have when interviewing people if you had a simple, easy-to-master system to make people feel *safe* when asking them something they didn't expect to tell you the truth about.
- Imagine if you were able to get what Lena calls the POIs (person of interest) in your personal or professional life to let their guard down, so they would feel at ease and give you exactly what you want: "honest answers."

That's why you may want to buy this book: you are about to be able to win people over and get "honest answers" from them—and so much more!

You may be wondering who I am. And why might my opinion about Lena Sisco's character or expertise matter to you.

My name is Janine Driver, and Anderson Cooper and NBC's *Today Show* have dubbed me the "Human Lie Detector." I've earned this reputation in part for being the CEO of the Body Language Institute, a business that helps people climb their career ladder more successfully through the study of nonverbal human behavior. I was the instructor in that advanced detecting deception, "train-the-trainer" class that Lena took back in 2013.

After seventeen years as an investigator for the Bureau of Alcohol, Tobacco, Firearms and Explosives (ATF), where I investigated firearms trafficking and illegal manufacturing of explosives cases, I retired at the age of thirty-eight to write a *New York Times* bestselling book called *You Say More Than You Think* (translated into fourteen languages). A couple of years later, I wrote the *Washington Post* bestseller *You Can't Lie to Me* (translated into nine languages). For decades, I've trained special agents and lawyers from the FBI, CIA, ATF, and numerous state and local law enforcement agencies, judges, as well as therapists, wardens, and patrol officers. I'm also a sales, leadership, HR, and communications consultant for such companies as Microsoft, Abbott Laboratories, Sales Force, Coca-Cola, Lockheed Martin, Comcast, and Equity Prime Mortgage (EPM).

Now that we've officially met, let's travel back to that 2013 class for a quick minute. I had no idea who Lena Sisco was, and I could've never guessed, in a million years, how deeply and profoundly she would catapult my interviewing and fact-finding skills, my reading people expertise, and ultimately . . . my life.

It wasn't until about an hour into class that I discovered Lena was a former US Navy intelligence officer and Marine Corps certified interrogator. I didn't know she worked for and with agencies such as the FBI, DIA, ONI (Office of Naval Intelligence), and NCIS.

I don't come from a heavy military family, so the only thing I knew about NCIS was what I had learned from watching a couple episodes of the fictional television program by the same name starring actor Mark Harmon. The *NCIS* series highlights a team of special agents investigating murder, espionage, and terrorism! Umm, ya, Lena was about to blow my mind.

Because it was a train-the-trainer course, this meant each student would have to present a one- to two-hour unique, dynamic, and interactive program on detecting deception. Lena started her presentation with a picture of the second airplane hitting the World Trade Center. Then, she dramatically paused, for about four seconds, before taking a deep breath and saying, "I woke up one day [pause], and my job was to figure out who did this. My name is Lena Sisco, and I'm a former Department of Defense certified military interrogator, where I interviewed members of Al-Qaeda and the Taliban at Gitmo." #MicDrop

We all were glued to every word Lena said next, as you'll be when you start reading this book. She had our undivided attention. We literally sat on the edge of our seats for the next 120 minutes.

Lena took the material she learned in class and combined it with, as you'll soon discover throughout the pages of this book, her extensive and impressive knowledge of human behavior, combined with her skills and abilities to detect deception and get to the truth. And had you been sitting toward the back of the room that late afternoon, you likely would have noticed me passing a handwritten note to my coinstructor, Chris Ulrich, fellow body language expert who had worked closely with top-level government officials for more than eighteen years. I wrote (pardon my language): "OMG! Lena is a badass! We need to invite her to be an instructor for our Body Language Institute courses immediately!"

That was the beginning of our almost decade-long personal and professional friendship. Since then, I've watched Lena do live and recorded interviews where she was able to get people to stop lying and provide her with "honest answers." I've seen Lena teach in small groups, where she has transformed people, just like you, into master interviewers. I've jumped to my feet, along with thousands of other people, at the end of her keynote presentations and her TEDx talk.

Lena and I have also been the go-to truth experts on endless television shows, and we had a popular video podcast with two other reading-people experts called *Profiler Task Force*, where we analyzed, with precision, influential leaders like RBG and notorious criminals such as Casey Anthony, Chris Watts, Barry Morphew, and the DC Snipers. We almost had our *own* television show on A&E (but a new executive came to town and cut all programs in the works).

Lena Sisco, my dear friend and colleague, has significantly changed not only my inter- and intrapersonal communication skills—she's impacted everyone with whom she's shared her tools. We've all gone through a transformation that includes a change in our decoding people mindset and how we approach working with people and negotiations. We have more extreme confidence, clarity in what we want to say, emotional control, and, of course, with Lena's elite human intelligence techniques, we are able to get information without asking for it.

When Lena asked me to write this foreword, I was honored, and I could not put this book down. I took twelve pages of notes in the blink of an eye, and I learned how to decode people in a different way than I had ever been taught before. Despite seeing Lena live for almost a decade, I still learned new tools through reading this book (laddering, how to use nonaccusatory language effectively, understanding personal drivers, motivators, and needs, and what Lena calls the "Motivation Equation").

This leads me to you! I'm so *excited* for you because it's now your turn to get a front-row seat to Lena Sisco's eliciting-the-truth program in this future bestseller, *Honest Answers*. When you read it, you'll automatically be connected with us, your fellow tribe of truth seekers.

Here's *exactly* what's in it for you if you choose to buy this book:

- You'll learn to accurately read people and adapt your language and your approach to build trust and ultimately grow sales.

- You'll discover how to prime people to tell the truth and stop deception in its tracks (and prevent over 89 percent of hiring mistakes!).
- You'll be equipped to build a culture of honesty, mutual respect, and psychological safety so your team feels safe and secure, which reduces turnover.

From one page to the next, Lena will generously share with you everything from why being the "nice guy" or "nice gal" always wins to how you can easily plan, prep, and practice your newfound tools. Through a series of exercises, Lena will guide you on how to build rapport in five minutes or less, understand personal drivers, motivators, and needs (this rocked my world), and master your questioning techniques. Lena will also cheer you on as you discover how to elicit information without asking for it and overcome conversational challenges, all while you build your empathic negotiation skills toolbox. Before you know it, you'll know how to handle the breaking point, decode body language accurately, and spot deceptive statements almost as well as a special agent!

In conclusion, I've been practicing Lena's techniques, outlined in this book, on my three sons (shh) in the last month, and the results have led me to call and email all my clients. I've primed them to get ready to buy this book for their sales, leadership, and HR teams as soon as it hits shelves because I have never, in the span of my training-filled career, read a more valuable book on how to get "honest answers" from people.

PREFACE

A S A NAVY Intelligence Specialist in 1999, I attended the Marine Corps Interrogation Prisoners of War School. Upon completion, I was a certified Department of Defense military interrogator. In 2003, I got to use my interrogation skills when I deployed to Camp Delta in Guantanamo Bay, Cuba, to interrogate members of Al-Qaeda and the Taliban. During that time, I discovered something invaluable about human nature: if you are nice and respectful to people, they tend to reciprocate in kind no matter what the circumstances are. My approach to interrogation at GTMO was to do something unexpected to get the truth: give respect, build rapport, and instill hope. Instead of preying on fear, I took advantage of trust. It was at this time I began to structure a rapport-based, nonaccusatory interviewing method that involved both direct and indirect techniques to get honest information. I am going to share that method and those techniques with you in this book.

I believe that once you have mastered the techniques and the science, interviewing becomes an art. You can gracefully and confidently control any conversation while gaining the other person's trust. And this does not mean you have to be a pushover or a patsy. In fact, you need to be quite the opposite; you can be austere and firm with a smile. I experienced multiple successes during my time as a military interrogator and collected actionable high-value intelligence because I knew how to talk to people. I knew human behavior and how the slightest change in my vocabulary, pitch, tone of voice, posture, and facial expression could have a massive impact on someone from whom I wanted to get the truth but who didn't want to give it to me.

Since leaving GTMO, I have been interrogating and interviewing various individuals in numerous settings, perfecting my strategy for winning over people and collecting pertinent data. Over the years, I have learned through trial and error what I believe is the most effective communication practices when it comes to interviewing and negotiating to obtain truthful information. After reading this book, I am confident you will have the knowledge to do the same.

Before we dive in, I need to explain that in the following chapters I will be using vernacular that may be unfamiliar to you. So allow me to take this opportunity to introduce you to a few terms. First, you will see the initialism "POI," which stands for "person of interest," to represent any person you are interviewing or negotiating with. A POI can be a witness, suspect, detainee, source, hostage, patient, job applicant, peer, colleague, stakeholder, even your teenager. Then I will outline what others have labeled "the SISCO method" of interviewing and negotiating.

Let me quickly define the SISCO interview method: SISCO stands for Strategic Interviewing Skills and Competencies; and obviously, it is my last name. My method embodies competencies that should be adopted as a procedure in every interview you conduct. My six core competencies are:

1. Apply non-accusatory questioning techniques including elicitation to create a safe environment for POIs to tell the truth by instilling hope instead of futility, building rapport, gaining trust, and being empathetic and nonjudgmental.
2. Think strategically to obtain not just a confession but truthful information, motivations, and intent.

3. Remain objective and aware to enhance focus, concentration, emotional control, and observation skills while eliminating assumptions, biases, and subjectivity.

4. Avoid the misinformation effect and false confessions.
5. Use the "Don't Tell, Ask" practice; never tell your POI what they did or why they did it if you do not know.
6. Detect and assess to the best of your ability both verbal and nonverbal deceptive indicators.

When you use my method, you are focusing on the human-to-human relationship first and getting the information second. The information will come if you have a strong understanding of human behavior. When you do, almost any adversarial opponent will succumb to rapport attempts. When you are conversing with agitated POIs, it can become a game of mental sparring. If the interviewer acquires pertinent information from the POI, it is their win; if the POI can withhold relevant information, it is the POI's win. My method aims at eliminating the adversarial mental sparring postures resulting in a win/win situation, or at least what appears to be a win/win situation to the POI. Any negotiator will tell you that in order to have a successful negotiation, you must enter the discussion thinking win/win; what do I want, what do *they* want, and how can we both get it? Interviewing is a negotiation; as the interviewer, I want the truth and the POI wants *something* in order to give it up. You will learn how to find this out in chapter 4, which is about discovering personal drivers and needs.

You can use the techniques outlined in this book in various circumstances and environments. Whether you are vetting potential new hires, interviewing employees regarding an equal opportunity issue or a workers' compensation case, eliciting facts from potential clients to generate validated leads, questioning a firm's accounting officer during a financial audit, negotiating with a seller, or questioning a suspect regarding a crime, use this book as your manual for planning and controlling your dialogue. These techniques can even help you elicit the truth from patients when trying to determine what is ailing them.

I have used my six core competencies in interviewing and negotiating while wearing many hats: as an interrogator, as an expert witness interviewing litigants, during fact-finding missions as a certified organizational change management specialist, and during informal coaching sessions. It is helpful when coaching others because when you coach you are not offering advice on fixing issues. In most instances, you won't have the expertise to do so. Coaches ask a series of thought-provoking interrogative questions to help the coachee further explore and define the situation so that they can come up with the best solutions on their own.

There was a time where my interviewing skills unexpectedly became a great asset for me. An organization tasked me to perform a gap analysis for a large government agency to help them with an organizational change management issue. This agency had undergone a significant cultural change; they went from being the customer to providing customer service out of a necessity to keep their mission funded. (And if I mentioned this agency, you would all know who it is! That's why I cannot.) I devised a plan to capture specific information from the workforce about organizational change management. After briefing my idea to the agency's senior executives, they scheduled interviews between their employees and me. I had four days to interview as many employees as I could, both at the location I was physically at and at another site virtually. Because time was a critical factor, I had to make sure every interview was effective. That meant my conversations had to be clear and concise, and I had to control them to extract the pertinent information. My nonaccusatory strategic interviewing skills allowed me to connect with the employees and gain their trust. I was shocked at how much they trusted me and how much they opened up to me, even about sensitive topics. I made sure to keep to a schedule, be clear in my questions, and communicate the reason for the interview. I listened to them attentively and answered any questions they had for me openly and honestly. I built rapport, gained their trust, and in the end, gathered so much information that the project went beyond the scope of my initial mission, creating a follow-on project. This is how I know my interviewing skills will transform your lives. Although most of my interview training today is with law enforcement, it has proven successful in many arenas, and I am confident it will bring you success in your world. In order to get honest answers you must use the techniques outlined in this book in conjunction with what you will learn about human behavior. Know this for certain: no one will be honest with you if they don't want to be. I will teach you techniques that take a person from not wanting to share to willingly telling the truth.

So that you can use this book as a guide, I have created activities at the end of most chapters to help you practice these new skills and techniques. Use these activities every time you plan, prepare, and practice for an interview or negotiation. These assignments will help you improve your overall interpersonal communication skills as well as enhance your emotional intelligence. Let's face it. As humans, we should always be students of those two areas.

This book will provide easy-to-understand concepts and processes, backed by research and years of experience. Most important, it will teach you how to apply them in your world. At the end of this book, I will provide you with an interview outline in Appendix A, called the Interview Flow. I have been asked many times about what my "flow"— which has proven successful for me time and time again—is during the interview process. Appendix B gives you a comprehensive interview checklist you can use before any interview, and Appendix C has the answers to all of the activities.

The interviewing skills I will share with you have helped me successfully facilitate, train, coach, and mentor other people. They have helped me be successful as an entrepreneur and businesswoman, and they have helped me help others become successful in their endeavors. Mostly, they have helped me be successful in putting criminals behind bars and keeping people safe.

You are reading this book because you decided to further your learning journey, and I know you will. This book will help you be successful in any type of information exchange. You will know what to say, how to say it, and how to get the honest answers you deserve.

● ● ●

"I am not a product of my circumstances.
I am a product of my decisions."

—STEPHEN COVEY

HONEST
ANSWERS

1

WHY BEING THE "NICE GUY" ALWAYS WINS

A LL MY LIFE, I found it easy to be the one in control and to make demands. I can be bossy and a little insensitive at times. I am an ENTJ, which according to the Myers-Briggs Type Indicator personality assessment, stands for Extroverted, Intuitive, Thinking, Judging. Now, there are many people, even colleagues of mine, who claim that the MBTI instrument is inaccurate. I firmly believe in its accuracy, and it has significantly expanded my knowledge of human behavior. I will leave the decision on believing or disbelieving up to you. However, I want to say that ENTJ suits me exactly. Being an Extrovert (E) who prefers activity and a lot of outside stimuli influences how I come across to others. Sometimes I appear to be too loud, talkative, pushy, and overbearing. I may also come across as the person who has to have all the attention and who likes to take center stage. Scoring high as an Intuitive (N) person who prefers to take information in conceptually and is comfortable working with theories and ideas can make me come across as having my head in the clouds and unclear in my communication. I also become impatient and frustrated when someone forces me to follow procedures. Being a Thinker (T) who prefers to make decisions based on facts and analysis more than how it affects people can make me come across as insensitive and unempathetic. And scoring as a Judging (J) person who prefers to organize their world with checklists can make me come across as inflexible and a micromanager. My personality preferences affect how I communicate with others, and so do yours. Have you ever considered how your personality either hindered or fostered your communication practices in your past relationships? The effect can be devastating. Let's say I am communicating with someone who prefers to make decisions based on how the outcome will affect other people, which according to MBTI would make them a "Feeler" (F). The Feeler may be offended when I make a decision based solely on facts and data, even if my intention is not to offend anyone. When this happened to me in the past, my younger, more immature self would think, "I'm not here to be your friend; I am here to make decisions to help you be safe and successful. I didn't intend to offend you, so if you feel offended, you will have to deal with it." Now, my more learned and mature self cringes at those past thoughts, and as a result, I have changed the way I think to, "If I offended someone, even if unintentionally, then it is up to me to figure out how not to offend people when I make decisions." That conscious decision to change my thoughts came from maturing my emotional intelligence and practicing mindfulness techniques.

We all have inherent personality preferences, thankfully! How boring would the world be if we were all alike? As a result, however, we can sometimes clash when managing a project, leading a team, and even conducting an interview. People who have a high level of emotional intelligence know that they cannot expect to talk others out of feeling the way they feel. We can change how we communicate with others, both verbally and nonverbally: the words that we use, our tone of voice, our inflection, and our body language. For example, we cannot expect someone to be agreeable when we say, "We need to talk," especially if we have our hands on our hips and our facial expression is leaking anger.

You may have heard the expression "perception is reality." Well, it's false. If perception were reality, it wouldn't be called "perception." Perceptions can become a reality when we lack the information to disprove them. Perceptions are just beliefs, and beliefs are only thoughts that we keep thinking over and over. My dear friend Ali Deuso told me that. She is a life coach who specializes in positive thought work to overcome disabling and sometimes debilitating issues we experience in life. Unfortunately, because we tend to hold our beliefs close to our heart, we often get defensive and become upset when they are challenged. Who do we usually blame in this situation? Not ourselves! We usually blame the other person for coming across as accusatory or rude even when they didn't know they were. It is easier to be the victim than it is to take responsibility for our perceptions. Let's face it, sometimes we do not realize how we come across to others. A good way to find out is to ask someone and hear the feedback without getting upset and taking it personally.

A couple of years after I graduated from interrogation school, I found myself interrogating detainees at Camp Delta in Guantanamo (GTMO) Bay, Cuba. I worried that I had to be "touchy-feely" to build rapport, and that did not come naturally to me because of my personality preference, nor did empathy. While in GTMO, I realized that being nice does not mean you have to be "touchy-feely." Being kind does not mean you cannot be confident. Being nonaccusatory does not mean you cannot be in control. Being nonjudgmental does not mean you cannot tell someone that what they did was wrong and as a result, they will be held accountable for their decisions. Being nice means practicing empathy and respecting another person's humanity even if you intend to send them to prison for the rest of their life. You do not want to be aggressive, but you can be assertive. Being assertive involves channeling your feelings into doing something productive rather than acting instinctively.

6

In my years of training people in interrogation and interviewing, I have realized that many individuals falsely associate being kind and respectful with being a pushover. That is not the case. Interviewers cannot be patsies. They have to be in control. But they have to be respectful at the same time. My husband, a colonel in the Marine Corps, says, "Do not mistake my kindness for weakness." Here are five techniques to use to maintain respect and authority while still being kind:

1. *Stand your ground—with a smile.* Do not let the person you are interviewing take over the interview. As the interviewer, you control the questions, the conversation, the timing, and the overall environment. Having control does not mean you cannot smile and be pleasant.

2. *Be empathetic, not sympathetic, when the time is right.* Empathy creates a deeper connection. Sympathy can come across as insincere. You also do not want to be sympathetic to a person who just committed intentional homicide. However, you can be empathetic, which will allow you to remain nonjudgmental and nonaccusatory.

3. *Having rapport does not mean you cannot discuss difficult topics.* As an interviewer, you will most likely have to talk about uncomfortable issues. In my line of work, I have to talk about crimes, criminal evidence, lying, and cheating. I can still do that while having rapport, by remaining nonaccusatory and nonjudgmental. I am also aware of my body language, facial expressions, demeanor, language, and tone of voice. I often tell the people I am interviewing that I am not there to judge them, just to get the information.

4. *Do not be afraid to call out the elephant in the room.* For example, if the person you are interviewing is starting to get visibly angry and defensive, shuts down, and refuses to talk, do not be afraid to address it. Their anger is the elephant in the room, and everyone can see, sense, and feel it. Address the

elephant. If you ignore it, the angry person may feel like they got a little win over you because they got away with being angry at you. When addressing anger in particular, I want you always to remember this golden rule: never tell a person how they feel, even if you can accurately read their facial expressions and their body language. It will only create a reason for them to become defensive and deny your accusation. Think of a time when someone told you how you were feeling. If someone says to me, "You look upset," if I wasn't upset then, I am now!

5. *Be done when you want to be done.* If you have the time, resources, and logistics, end the interview when you are ready to end it. Do not terminate the interview because the person you are interviewing is beginning to get argumentative, or is bored, or wants to be somewhere else. If you terminate the interview before getting the information you want, that is their win, not yours. They took control of the interview. Do not be done exploiting the topic because the interviewee wants to be done talking about it. You can say things such as, "I still don't feel I have enough information; I am still unclear about . . ." and continue asking questions. If the interviewee tells you they want to cease the interview, ask them why. This will keep them talking and prolong the interview. You may even get them to want to keep talking. Remember the *Columbo* television show and the detective's famous technique? He would say he was done asking questions, but he kept right on asking them, and people would fall for it. They believed he was finished gathering evidence, so what was the harm in answering a few more questions since they weren't part of his official interview? When I was an interrogator in GTMO, after I terminated the interview and was waiting for a guard to come take the detainee back to his cell, I thought, "Why waste the opportunity to get more information?" I

wouldn't take notes, but I would keep interrogating. And I would get some juicy leads in those last few minutes of conversation. Why? Because to the detainees, it wasn't part of the interrogation. My interpreters called me Columbo.

When you treat people with respect, they will treat you with respect. It is an example of quid pro quo, the Latin phrase that means, "this for that." If you can remain friendly and respectful, you are exhibiting emotional control. You will not become reactive to situations or to what others say. Instead, you will act with intention, owning everything you do and say.

Here are a few techniques to work on your emotional control. First, do not beat yourself up for feeling an emotion, even anger or jealousy. As a human, you will feel emotions. And although you cannot control your emotions, you can control your response to them. Let me explain this with a situation most of us have been in: being cut off in traffic. How did you feel? Most of us get angry. I curse and make hand gestures I shouldn't. What is it that made me so mad? It wasn't "because someone cut me off." What angered me were my thoughts about being cut off. Most of us immediately think, "How dare they cut me off! Who do they think they are? Where they are going is not more important than where I need to go. They could have hit me!" These thoughts create our anger. If we change our thoughts, we can change our emotional reactions. The next time someone cuts you off in traffic, instead of thinking the usual thoughts, try to think differently. Think to yourself, "I wonder if they are rushing to the hospital. What if they just didn't see me?" We tend to be more empathetic and less angry when we think about these types of thoughts. If we change our thoughts, we can change our reactions. This phenomenon is similar to what Stephen Covey calls paradigm shifts, when something happens to shift our reactionary thoughts and behaviors.

I recently hosted a webinar called "Practice ESP to Perfect Any Conversation." The initialism ESP does not stand for extrasensory perception. In this case, it means "Embrace self-discovery, Seek knowledge, and Practice empathy." ESP is a mental checklist to hold myself accountable for my actions and behaviors, especially during emotional and confrontational conversations. When I become emotional and reactive, it is usually because I am not practicing one of those elements. When I am in a conversation that becomes emotionally intense, I analyze how I am coming across to the other person as objectively as possible. You need to Embrace self-discovery to understand your personality traits and how others perceive you; your words, tone of voice, body language, communication style, and decision-making style. Then I lean into Seeking knowledge. I make a mental list of the known facts and another list of the information I made up to fill in the gaps. Let's face it, as humans we tend to make up a story if we do not have the facts. And finally, I Practice empathy.

During an interrogation or an interview, the conversation may get heated or hostile. The interviewee could say something to push your buttons and upset you, intentionally or not. We do not want to lose control of our emotions because we could lose rapport, our credibility, and potentially lifesaving information. In my years of interrogating and interviewing, the biggest lesson I have learned is captured in the saying "You attract more bees with honey than vinegar." This philosophy has become the backbone of my interviewing method.

● ● ●

"Trust is the glue of life.
It's the most essential ingredient in effective
communication. It's the foundational principle
that holds all relationships."

—STEPHEN COVEY

ACTIVITY

Become more self-aware to increase your situational awareness. Use this space to answer the following questions in order:

- How do you come across to others in your personal and professional relationships? (verbally, nonverbally)
- What is your personality style—your traits and characteristics. If you have never taken a personality assessment, I encourage you to take a free assessment at 16personalities.com.
- How do you usually build rapport with others?
- What is your primary purpose for establishing rapport with others?
- Describe two situations when you were empathetic or practiced empathy. How did you feel?
- What angers you?
- How can you change your thoughts so that you do not become angered?
- What are your negative emotional reactionary responses to certain types of people and situations?
- What are your positive emotional reactionary responses to certain types of people and situations?
- What do you do to be authentic? (not reacting to people or situations and doing or saying things you wished you had not)
- Think of the last time you had a conflict with someone. Look back and objectively analyze what happened. Could you have done anything differently? Write it down. When we write things down, we tend to

remember them better. If it involves changes we want to make, we'll be more able to commit to them in the future.

- When did you last experience a paradigm shift? Describe the situation and the outcome. How did it help you, or how can it help you in similar future situations?

2

PLAN, PREP, AND PRACTICE

YOU'VE HEARD THE phrase "Practice makes perfect." It does. You have to practice your interviewing skills to get comfortable with them, gain confidence in your interview style, and, most importantly, get to the point where your techniques come naturally to you. Practice will help you think on your feet, a necessary skill because interviewing is like a mental sparring game. When you practice, plan for all of the "what-ifs" that can happen to handle those circumstances with ease when they do occur, because they will. When preparing for a successful interview, you want to consider your verbal, nonverbal, and emotional responses to certain situations. In this chapter, I will teach you how to practice and how to plan out the "what-if" scenarios to increase your awareness and agility. You will learn to become proactive instead of reactive.

• • •

WHERE DO YOU BEGIN?

In your job/role/position, consider the types of interviews you will be conducting. You may be interviewing to collect information from an individual, collect information from a group, screen people for employment or security purposes, test individuals regarding a particular skill set, or determine how people act under pressure. Consider your objective(s) and whether you will be conducting a tactical or strategic interview. Now consider the personality profile of the people you will typically be interviewing. Will your interviewees be guarded, talkative, cooperative, belligerent, doubtful, trusting, biased, unbiased, educated, or uneducated? (Later, I will discuss personality and communication preferences more in-depth so you can assess others' preferred styles of communicating and thinking. I will tell you why they are essential to know and how they can help you be more successful in your interviewing techniques.)

Will you be interviewing a female or a male? Consider how either will respond to you. As a female, it is easy for me to build rapport with either sex, but as a male, it may be more difficult to gain trust from a female in certain circumstances, especially if you are interviewing female victims of sexual abuse, assault, or human trafficking. It may sound corny, but women and men speak different languages. Men use fewer words to make a point and may come across to women as being too abrupt and harsh, even rude. Women use more words to make a point and may come across to men as too wishy-washy, emotional, and indecisive. Men tend to focus on logic and facts, while women tend to focus on feelings and human relations. Changing how you speak to the opposite sex can have a profound impact on how they perceive you. I know when I am trying to make a point to my husband, I leave out emotive words and keep the sentences short and to the point. He is a Marine, after all. (That is a joke. I have the utmost admiration for my husband and the Marines!)

Assess the POI's physical, mental, and emotional state. Cogitate it all and practice for it all! I like to practice for the worst-case scenario, then everything else will be a breeze. When I was interrogating detainees at Camp Delta, I would plan for how a member of the Taliban vs. a foreign fighter would respond to specific questions I would ask and topics I wanted to exploit. The reason why was that they had different knowledge, connections, and personal motivators for fighting. It would be impractical to approach them the same way. I would plan for the most formidable resistance and how I was going to persuade them to tell the truth—or "break," as we called it. So, when the resistance came, I had techniques I could use to get them to want to be truthful and honest with me. I would plan for other circumstances, too, such as: What if they tried to harm me physically? What if they refused to say anything and just sat there in silence (and they did!)? What if they claimed the guards on cellblock were mistreating them? What if they told me, "There is nothing you can do to make me talk"? I came up with as many different scenarios as I could, with as many kinds of personalities, to fully prepare myself with a plan for each, so they didn't catch me off guard. And for your information, when they did sit in silence, I would sit in silence with them until it became so awkward that they would say something. When they did, I had won the battle of wits! And then I would ask an open-ended question to get them to talk, such as, "Why do you want to keep sitting here in silence?" You have to outwit your opponent.

To help prepare yourself, play your own devil's advocate. In a sense, you will be role-playing with yourself, being the interviewer and the interviewee. What would work and what wouldn't? And don't go easy on yourself. What could you say? What shouldn't you do? Set realistic goals. For example, my first goal may be to get someone comfortable enough to want to talk with me. My second goal may be to get someone to trust me, and my third may be to get them to speak truthfully.

Individuals who study martial arts practice the same way. They are continually thinking of the "what-ifs." What if a person tries to punch me in the face? How would I block and counter? In my inter-rogation training, we trained for the worst-case scenarios. Our role-players acted like the most uncooperative, belligerent prison-ers they could. In the real world, I have never encountered the level of difficulty I trained for, which made the training so effective. I re-member thinking after my first real-world interrogation, "That was just like training, but way easier." If you don't train like this, you will not be prepared.

When you role-play interview scenarios against yourself, speak out loud. It will make the situation appear more realistic, and it will get your mouth and your voice used to speaking "canned" responses that you will want to use when the time comes in a real-word interview. It will also allow you to hear how you sound. Do you sound empathetic, aggressive, condescending, or confident? Doing this will help you think on your feet because you will have already rehearsed what you want to say and how you will say it. I used to come up with about two to three responses if a detainee would say to me:

- "I'm not going to talk." ("I can't make you talk, nor do I intend to try to, but why wouldn't you want to get out of your cell even if it meant talking to me?" To get them talking, always ask interrogative questions that begin with who, what, where, when, why, and how.)
- "I don't have to answer your questions." ("No, you don't. But let me ask you, why don't you want to answer them?" And that would usually get them talking.)
- "I want to go back to my cell." ("If I let you go back now, you will be called into interrogation by someone else. I want to hear your side of the story without judgment. How do you feel about that?")
- "You can't help me." ("How do you know that?" or "Why do you think that?" or "What help do you want?")
- "Why should I talk to you?" ("Why shouldn't you?")
- "Why should I trust you?" ("Why shouldn't you?" or "Because

I am open and honest with you. But I can stop if you aren't willing to be open and honest with me. So, why should I trust you?")

In law enforcement, you may want to plan responses for when:

- You are asked by a potential suspect, "Don't I get a lawyer or something?"
- Your seasoned criminals are not interested in being honest, only in what their statement will cost them in jail time.
- You have to talk to teenagers who come across as not caring about anything or anyone.
- You have to question a juvenile who fears authority figures.
- You have to interview someone where there are bystanders nearby.

In the business world, you may want to plan responses for when:

- A potential customer says, "Let me think about it some more before I commit to buying."
- An existing client says, "Your competitor has a better rating, so I'm thinking of leaving you and going with them."
- A contractor says, "I saw your last quarter figures, and I don't know if your company can support our clients long-term."

In the private sector, you may want to plan responses for when:

- You have to conduct a phone interview.
- You have to work with an interpreter.
- You have to interview someone who tells you they are pressed for time.

Let's say you are an executive recruiter. You are interviewing a potential job candidate who has, up until now, said they are fully committed to quitting their current employment to take a position with your client's company. But for the past week they have not answered or returned your calls. Perhaps they are not as committed as they expressed, and they are getting cold feet. Or maybe they were offered a pay raise to stay with their current employer. What will you say to them to find out the truth?

What if you are a realtor and a potential home buyer tells you that they have decided now is not the time for them to move, and they are going to wait to see if the rates are better in six months? What if you are an HR manager investigating an Equal Opportunity complaint, and the employee who made the complaint tells you they want to recant but will not tell you why? What if a potential client told you they were interested in your services and when you follow up with them a week later, they tell you they have to get their director's approval? These are "what-if" scenarios to prepare you to know what to say and how to say it confidently. The techniques in this book will teach you how to do that.

Thinking about these scenarios and planning how to respond will help you handle them efficiently and effectively without getting stumped or startled. The moment you show any hesitation or doubt, especially in an adversarial interview, is the moment your adversary wins. Remember this, confidence attracts, insecurity detracts. You must be confident, and your confidence level will come with planning, preparing, and practicing. Practice every day, and I guarantee you will be thankful for the confidence, ability, and flexibility you will gain.

We prepare for interviews so we can avoid surprises. Surprises can catch us off guard, which may lead to increased anxiety and frustration in both ourselves and our interviewees. To help us avoid surprises, we should know and understand the purpose of the interview and how we will achieve success.

To sum it up, there are four things you need to know to ensure a successful interview:

- Yourself
- Your information
- The person you are interviewing
- How you will get the information you need

KNOW YOURSELF

Awareness is critical in communication, whether you are trying to build rapport, liaise with professionals, detect deception, sell a product, manage a team, or be a virtuous parent. We all need enhanced communication skills in our everyday lives. Sometimes, however, our communication skills falter due to a lack of self-awareness and awareness of others. You may be unaware that you project yourself in a way that has negative consequences, such as being condescending, overbearing, argumentative, or too direct. On the flip side, you may come across as too meek, insecure, or submissive. Communication barriers can form when others do not like how you come across, even if your intentions were the exact opposite of their perception. An interviewer's goal is to be likable. To do that, we have to know if the people we are interviewing perceive us as amiable and approachable or unpleasant and inhospitable.

Check in with yourself. What is your personality? How do you come across to others verbally and nonverbally? What are your emotional triggers? How do you handle change? What is your preferred communication style? You have to know yourself before you can get to know others. When you become aware of how you think, feel, act, react, make decisions, communicate, and handle change, you can better observe and assess others' preferences. You will naturally become more empathetic.

We have to allow people to exercise their personal preferences, especially if we don't want them to judge ours. Accept the diversity among those around you and learn to influence it instead of letting it control you. When you can open yourself up to allowing others to be who they are, you may even learn a thing or two from them and grow personally and professionally.

Another thing you should be aware of, aside from your personality preference, is your communication style preference. You may have more than one for different situations. I know my preferred communication style is predominantly directive in both my personal and professional life. Being directive has caused some strife. There is undoubtedly a time and place for a direct communication style, such as in a crisis, but it is not the best style for other situations such as making family plans. When communicating, my priorities are to get to the point and deliver a clear, concise message quickly. It is also to acquire clear, detailed information. I slip into "interrogation mode" sometimes when I am trying to get to the bottom of something, but in doing so, I can make some people feel uncomfortable. I can come across as too demanding and insensitive. Because I know this, I can identify when I need to adjust my communication and possibly mirror the other person's preferred style. Making simple changes in your words can have a significant impact on whether or not someone trusts you. For example, when you tell a person that they can't do something, they will most likely become defensive. But when you say to a person what they can do, they are more prone to listen and agree with you. I will discuss this more when I cover how to change negative language to positive and accusatory to nonaccusatory in chapter 3. Being aware of your personality and your preferred communication style can significantly increase your chances of building rapport, gaining trust, and ultimately getting the person you are interviewing to open up and tell the truth. The good news is that it is not difficult to increase our self-awareness.

Self-awareness is crucial for effective communication, especially during interviews. We should all be aware of how we look and sound when we are communicating. We should consider our postures, gestures, facial expressions, stance, and overall composure and demeanor. Think of your communication style and whether you tend to use more directive language or social language. What tone does your voice have? What pitch? What is your rate of speech? Reflect on your thoughts, which are affected by your biases and expectations, and, of course, your personality preferences. Even take note of your hygiene, dress, and overall appearance before you conduct an interview. Why? Because just as people judge books by their covers, they judge people by what they look like and how they sound.

Knowing yourself also includes considering how you feel in a particular environment. The noise level or the space's role/use may unconsciously influence your behavior or your interviewee's behavior. For example, suppose your manager calls you into their office. You might feel uncomfortable and therefore not as open in your communication as you would be in a common area such as a conference room. While I was interrogating at Camp Delta, I discovered that the detainees were much more relaxed walking to and from the interrogation room than actually being in the interrogation room. I would be walking with the detainee from their cell to the interrogation trailers with two guards and the interpreter, in the hot Caribbean sun, having an easygoing, interactive conversation until we arrived at the air-conditioned interrogation room. As soon as the guards left, the detainee closed up. When I realized this, I summoned the guards, and we went walking outside around the camp as I conducted my interrogation.

KNOW YOUR INFORMATION

I have a rule: if I do not know something, I ask. And I certainly do not pretend to know something that I don't.

If you choose to bluff, someone may call you out. Then you will lose credibility and, ultimately, the information you need. In interrogation school, we learned an approach technique called "We Know All." It's a bluffing technique. You pretended to know more than you did, and you used ruses to justify how much you seemed to know. For instance, cops and interrogators use the "padding the file" technique. That is when you have a file on a detainee or suspect, and you pad it, physically, with lots of papers and photos that do not pertain to anything. It just looks as though you have a lot of information on them. When the detainee/suspect sees all the information in the file, they may become concerned and confess everything. Some people fall for this technique, but most do not. And if they call your bluff, you will be the loser in that game. I don't like to lose, so if I don't know something, I ask for it. Keep in mind that we give away what we do not know by asking for it, so be wary of tipping your hand. My favorite technique in place of the "We Know All" approach is the "What do you think?" approach. That's when I ask questions such as: "What do you think we know about . . ." "If someone told us already . . ." "If we have surveillance on you . . ." "If you already admitted to the crime by saying . . ." "If we bring in someone who knows you . . ." "If your buddies found out . . ." You can keep going on and on. This plants a seed of doubt in the person you are interviewing. They will begin to doubt themselves, not you, regarding whether or not they can get away with lying.

On the flip side, if you have a lot of available information from reports, evidence, surveillance, snitches, or any trusted source, then, by all means, use the "We Know All" approach. To use it effectively, know when and how to present the information you know. Do not offer it too quickly or easily; use it methodologically. This technique is called Strategic Use of Evidence (SUE). Give the person a chance to come clean first. If they resist, then slowly begin introducing the evidence. Start by trickling in all the information you know little by little so that even the smallest piece of information, when stacked up, seems more meaningful and incriminating. It makes the person you are interviewing feel you already know everything, so there is no way out of telling the truth. Another useful technique you can use regarding evidence, especially if you have physical evidence, is to make the POI touch it, if applicable. For instance, photos are great to hand to people or place before them, so they cannot avoid the pictures. A guilty person will not want to look at the photo, much less touch it.

A note of caution: if you are too focused on evidence and introduce it too early in the interview, your attention will be on the evidence and not the interview process. You could tunnel vision on the evidence and tune out what the POI is or is not saying. Focusing on evidence may also bias your questions, and you could lose your ability to remain objective. You may also cause your POI to focus on the evidence, making them repeat information back to you instead of providing new information. To avoid this, hold on to evidence as long as possible. It can increase the POI's anxiety because they may focus on what information you know, which could increase their cognitive load and cause them to leak more deceptive indicators. Using SUE can also help you avoid contaminating the POI's memory. This is known as the misinformation effect.

The misinformation effect occurs when a person is presented with information after an event that affects their memory trace of the event. Cognitive psychologist Elizabeth Loftus is a leading expert on the misinformation effect and eyewitness memory. According to the white paper "Creating New Memories That Are Quickly Accessed and Confidently Held," which Loftus coauthored with Karen Donders, Hunter G. Hoffman, and Jonathan W. Schooler, "Information presented after an event can change a person's report of that event. When the new information is misleading, it can produce errors in that report." You may not intentionally mislead a suspect or a witness, but you may inadvertently misinform them and create a new false memory. You may be wondering how this is even possible. Memory has a limited capacity for storing information and reconstructing encoded messages. We encode information in schemas, which is a fancy word for a memory blueprint. Biases, assumptions, expectations, inattentional blindness, and subjective interviewing can change our

23

blueprint, affect how we perceive things, and alter our memories of events. Another phenomenon known as interference occurs when some memories interfere with the retrieval of other memories. When you have similar memories, interference can make it hard to distinguish between them.

Our goal as interviewers is to collect as much accurate information as possible. That can be a tedious task, especially when we have to deal with schemas and biases, long-term and short-term memory.

The misinformation effect can be very dangerous. It can lead to a false confession of a crime that one didn't commit and you can send an innocent person to prison or let a guilty individual go free. Be aware of how you present information, and avoid biased statements and hypothetical scenarios. The more objective you are, the more you decrease the possibility of the misinformation effect.

KNOW THE PERSON YOU ARE INTERVIEWING

That sounds a bit like Captain Obvious, but you need to take this a level deeper. Put yourself in their shoes. Think like them. (I will discuss personal drivers, motivators, and needs in chapter 4.) Have you researched and analyzed previous reports or personal accounts from other people who have observed, handled, lived with, arrested, and talked to the POI? If you are interviewing a new hire, have you spoken with their colleagues or previous employers to find out information not on their resume? If you are interviewing a student about a bullying accusation, have you talked with other teachers and students to collect data on observable events? The more you know about the person you are interviewing, the better your chances are of building rapport, gaining trust, planning for the "what-ifs," formulating practical questions, using effective questioning techniques, and having a successful interview. This level of planning will also help you make the best use of your time.

Aside from biographical data, the circumstances of the interview, and the objective(s) of the interview, some questions to consider before you interview someone so you can get to know them on a deeper level include:

- How do they feel about being interviewed?
- What emotions might they be experiencing now, during, and after the interview?
- What information do they know, or should they know?
- What topics do you think they will feel comfortable/uncomfortable talking about?
- What is their perception of you? Of the interview? Of the situation?
- What will make them like you? Be interested in you? Want to open up and talk to you?
- How are you going to gain their trust?
- How are you going to act around them? What will be your demeanor and your personality?
- What is their personality profile?
- What communication style will you use?
- What is their communication style?
- What topics will upset them?
- What subjects will be taboo or sensitive to them?
- What is their education level/experience?
- What are their likes and interests?
- What language(s) do they speak?
- What family/friends do they have? What do they say about the POI?

When you know your POI, you can build better rapport, earning their trust and honesty. You will also understand what types of questions to ask and topics to broach. You will know what to say and what *not* to say. You will be better able to pick up on deception.

KNOW HOW YOU WILL GET THE INFORMATION

Finally, before you interview a POI, you should know how you will obtain the information you need. Consider how much time you have to interview and then plan out your interview strategy. Outline your goals and objectives. Include the topics you plan to exploit, the questions you plan to ask, and the questioning techniques you plan to use, which you will learn about in chapter 5. You may want to avoid questions because your POI is nervous or guarded, and as such, you will plan to use elicitation to get answers. You will also need to plan how you will act; what will be your demeanor, personality, and tone of voice? If you know your POI, you will have a sense of how to act. For example, I often use humor to build rapport. It works with my personality and is a very productive tool for me.

However, there are some people that I will not be able to connect with using humor because of their personality or the context of the situation. As a result, I need another approach to make the POI feel comfortable with me. Sometimes I go into the interview sounding more authoritative and assertive. Sometimes I am more soft-spoken and empathetic. Sometimes I go into an interview upbeat, extroverted, and naive. Sometimes I am focused on making the other person feel good, and other times I am focused on getting that person to realize they cannot lie to me because I know how to detect deception. Plan out how you are going to build rapport and gain the POI's trust thoroughly. Do not leave this up to chance. If you are not prepared, you may leak insecurity and lose your credibility.

When you are drafting your outline, make sure it is flexible, meaning you have room to switch up your tactics. If your initial interview strategy does not quite hit the mark, and you have no backup plan, it won't be easy to create a new objective on the fly. When you prepare your interview strategy, prepare multiple designs that will fit different situations, personalities, and goals. This way you can keep your confidence and credibility.

Avoid reading off your list of questions. You may come across as robotic, insensitive, and uncaring. Or you could tunnel vision around your questions and forget to listen to what the POI is saying. An information lead is a relevant topic or piece of information you were unaware of that a POI has. When I plan for an interview, I usually have a list of about five key topics with a few questions prepared for each, but I may exploit ten topics during the interview because of new leads. Your prepared questions are a guide to keep you on track while allowing you to maintain open awareness to hear new leads and openings to a new topic within a conversation. These openings are known as "conversational gates." Conversational gates are easier to exploit when the POI brings them up unwittingly. That is because if the interviewer introduces a new topic too abruptly, it could alert the POI and cause concern. The POI may wonder, "Why did the interviewer stop asking me questions about X and now wants to know about Y?" But if the POI brings up Y, or a topic related to Y, you can go through that "gate" and start talking about Y unassumingly.

When planning on how to get your information, you should use the hourglass technique to ease concerns and increase cooperation. This technique refers to when you start the interview at the macro level—the nonspecific part when you build rapport, gain trust, and talk about nonpertinent topics and generalities to influence the POI to be open, honest, and forthcoming. Avoid getting too specific or bringing up sensitive issues. Your focus at the beginning is to win them over. The macro level is an excellent time to use elicitation. Then you can ease into the micro level, get into specifics, and ask pertinent questions on sensitive topics. You will use effective questioning techniques and methods to detect deception. After you fully exploit all the information you need, bring it back out to the macro level again to close out the interview, leaving your POI relaxed and unassuming. At this point, you reinforce the rapport you built initially, ask them what you can do for them, and hand over control of the conversation to the interviewee. Let the POI ask you questions as you prepare them to be questioned by you or someone else again in the future. We want to use the hourglass technique because people usually remember the first few minutes and the last few minutes of each conversation. They typically have some trouble remembering or forget altogether what they discussed during the middle of the conversation. We don't want to end the interview leaving the POI with any ongoing concerns, doubts, anxiety, guilt, or other negative emotions, so we have to ensure we terminate the interview on a high note.

By now, you should feel assured about how to plan for your interview thoroughly. You have not only considered all of the logistics discussed in the last chapter, but you have done a deep-dive self-assessment, assessed the POI, gathered all the necessary information regarding the POI, strategically determined how you will use that information, and carefully planned out how you intend to collect the information. The next step is perfecting the first few minutes of your interview to build rapport so that you set the stage for victory.

Appendix B will give you a comprehensive checklist to incorporate all chapter material.

• • •

"By failing to prepare, you are preparing to fail."

—BENJAMIN FRANKLIN

3

HOW TO BUILD RAPPORT IN FIVE MINUTES OR LESS

F YOU WANT to accomplish your objectives and obtain the information you seek when interviewing and negotiating, rapport is necessary and critical. Rapport is not just getting someone to like you. It is the ability to think and feel like the other person and mirror their behaviors so that they become interested in us and wish to establish a relationship with us. The bond should become so strong that the other person feels better confessing to you than keeping a secret.

I have discovered that when you have a meaningful rapport with someone, you can get the truth from them, even if it comes with jail time. Most of us know how to build rapport with others, and we may even have go-to methods we use to persuade others to like us. In this chapter, I will share my go-to methods for establishing deep connections with the people I interview. I will describe what I consider to be the five most effective ways to connect with others:

• • •

1. Find common ground.
2. Mirror others' behaviors.
3. Change your language.
4. Assign a positive trait.
5. Ask for help.

But first I want to address empathy because empathy makes us proficient rapport builders. Empathy is when you see things from someone else's viewpoint. You imagine how they feel, what they may be going through, and how they were affected by decisions and situations. Find out their perspective on things so you can validate their feelings and emotions. Try to see the world through their lens. At the speed at which most of us communicate these days, we don't allow ourselves the time to do this. Not having empathy will hinder our ability to be sincere and credible while trying to establish a connection with others.

Stephen Covey advises, "Seek first to understand, then to be understood." All you have to do is listen to what others are communicating. Contain your biases, judgments, assumptions, and expectations. Refrain from making up a story when you do not have all of the facts. Ask questions to get the information you do not know and engage in reciprocity. If you make it known to the POI that you will take care of them, then they will take care of you. If you are up front, sincere, and honest with them, they will be that way for you. I call this the "quid pro quo" technique: treat others how you want to be treated. It will not work on everyone because some people have personal motivations, drivers, and personality disorders that supersede reciprocity. However, it still works on most because it is human nature to be nice to those who are nice to us. When we are nice to others, it will be difficult for them not to be nice back. The same thing goes for smiling; when you smile at others, they tend to smile back at you. Being nice to people who do not like you, who have insulted you, or who will not cooperate with you is not easy, but still necessary. I tell people I train that it costs nothing to be nice, yet it can get you everything. Always be nice, but do not be a pushover. There is a difference. Being respectful does not mean you will let others disrespect you. Be vulnerable, make mistakes, and admit to past failures; but still have confidence and authority. Truly confident people have no problem admitting to mistakes, whereas insecure people do. In place of confidence, insecure people will be arrogant, which they mistake for looking confident.

When we allow ourselves to become more empathetic, we can use the following rapport-building techniques with ease. The first and most straightforward technique you should use to connect with someone is to find common ground.

FIND COMMON GROUND

I start every interview thinking about finding the one thing the interviewee and I have in common. I believe the most effective way to gain someone else's interest so that they want to explore establishing a relationship with you is to exploit the similar-to-me bias and find out what you have in common. In my world, I could be interviewing a terrorist, a serial killer, a drug dealer, or a cheater. I am none of those things, but if I want a criminal to tell me where the next crime will take place or who the next victim will be, I have to think like them and be like them enough that they feel some connection with me. I am not saying that I will pretend to be a murderer; that would be ridiculous. But if I am talking to a suspect who feels the world has done him wrong and is angry at his circumstances, I will try to share something similar that I have experienced when I have felt the world did me wrong. I may embellish the story. I may even lie, but only about things I can say with sincerity and remember. As a rule, however, try not to bluff about your experiences. Coming across as insincere, fake, or a liar will ruin any chance of rapport and information.

The easiest way to find out what you have in common with someone is to share something about yourself. You want to use the similar-to-me bias to find out what you have in common so you can share similar experiences. Think quid pro quo, an elicitation technique that I will discuss in chapter 7. Elicitation is used in place of questions to elicit answers in an unassuming manner to promote a free-flowing dialogue, reduce stress and tension, and help build rapport. Some people refer to elicitation as an indirect questioning technique because you are not asking questions; you only make narrative statements to provoke a narrative response. In my view, elicitation is a brilliant way to find out the information you can't ask for because it may be too sensitive in nature.

Using quid pro quo, you can discover common ground and exploit the similar-to-me bias. To find commonalities, start with broad subjects and work to specifics. For example, you may both like sports and discover you like the same team. Think of how we make new friends. Usually, it begins with a commonality. Figure out a way to connect with your POI, even if it takes time and effort.

A few years ago, a private security firm based in Switzerland hired me to help them investigate a money laundering case. There were three of us conducting the investigation; me (an American), a female Russian investigator whom I'll call Anika, and an English citizen who was the president of the company; I'll call him Allan. We all met in Dubai to interview a Middle Eastern man (I'll call him Asim) about his role in the crime. The first time I met with this man in the ultramodern lobby of the Sofitel Hotel in Dubai, he would not even look me in the eye. He didn't know me, but he knew Anika and Allan, and he kept his attention on them. Asim was a large man dressed in a black suit and charcoal grey button-down shirt, with thick, black, slicked-back hair. We all sat on the plush aqua blue sofas in front of the floor-to-ceiling wall of windows.

The conversation between the four of us lasted about twenty-five minutes. We drank bottled water and nothing else. We offered Asim coffee and canapes, but he didn't accept. He did not want to be there. He joked with Allan but had little regard for Anika and me. I had no rapport with this guy, and the meeting ended. We were meeting him again the next afternoon, and I remember feeling determined to get his attention and connect with him. The next day, he arrived in the same lobby, right on time, with two other men dressed in light grey suits. Asim's entourage left his side when he saw us across the lobby, and we motioned for him to come over. We were all standing around the couches and chairs. We let him sit first. We had preplanned this so that wherever he sat, I could sit down next to him, and my colleagues could sit across from him. The first thing Asim said was that he didn't have a lot of time because he had a long flight the next day. I heard an opportunity to find common ground, so I took it. I chimed in and shared my experience about flying to Dubai from the United States just the day before. He looked at me and listened with his ears and eyes. He said, "Ah, then you know what it's like." So, I continued the dance and said, "Well, I was entertained by this movie I watched . . ." As I explained the premise of the movie, his eyes lit up, and now he turned his body to face mine. Our belly buttons were facing each other. (My friend and colleague Janine Driver calls this "naval intelligence.") I had his attention. To my luck and surprise, he had seen the movie and loved it. For the next five minutes, he and I laughed about the movie. Then he asked if we all wanted coffee. It was a little bit of luck, a lot of determination, and a lot of patience, but in the end I got what I wanted: rapport. We all sat and drank Americanos, and he agreed to take a polygraph for us. Never underestimate what rapport can do, and never give up trying to establish a connection with someone. You can find common ground with anyone.

Being similar to others is not just sharing the same likes and dislikes; it also includes personality, appearance, and how they speak. Rapport can be established merely by mirroring a person's posture, gestures, facial expressions, tone and pitch of their voice, words and phrases, breathing, and blink rate. This brings me to the second rapport-building method.

MIRRORING OTHERS' BEHAVIORS

Isopraxism is the technical term for when you display the same behaviors as the person with whom you are speaking. For example, if a person has their left leg crossed over their right, you will have your right leg crossed over your left; you are a mirror image of each other. Matching is when you display the same body posture that does not look like a mirror image. So, if a person has their chin resting in their right hand, you will rest your chin on your right hand. If you want to mirror or match but do not want to position your body language in the exact position of your interviewee, use a slight variation. For instance, if they have their chin resting in the palm of their hand, you may rest your chin on the backside of your hand or between your index finger and thumb. It is good to incorporate variations because you do not want to look like you are mimicking them. And make sure you do not mirror a gesture too quickly because that will also make you look like you are mimicking.

Mirroring and matching both require the conscious mind to study a person's behavior. The intent, however, is for mirroring to occur outside the conscious awareness of the other individual so that it comes across as unconscious behavior. To avoid making sudden movements, wait at least thirty seconds before trying to mirror/match the other person's behaviors and movements. If your actions are too immediate, you may risk the other person becoming aware of what you are doing, and you could draw unnecessary attention to yourself. Let's face it: if we catch someone mimicking us, it's annoying and a little creepy. But when we can look, sound, and act like another person, we create a feeling of being similar to them at an unconscious level.

When mirroring others' behaviors, you have to understand how to pace and lead. Pacing and leading refer to when the other person starts to mirror or match you unconsciously. When that happens, you have the ultimate unconscious connection. Try it out at work with a friend or colleague or at home with a family member. See if you can get another person to start mirroring or matching your body posture and gestures without them knowing. When they do, they are in tune with you. You can mirror and match a person over the phone as well. Simply match their vocabulary, speech rate, tone, pitch, and volume.

I find mirroring verbally is more natural and more effective than mirroring nonverbally. For instance, introverted people tend to speak softer and slower and think about what and how they want to say things before they say it. Being an extrovert, I talk loud and fast, and quite often put my foot in my mouth. So, when I converse with more introverted people, I change my verbal behaviors to match theirs. I have found that introverts feel more comfortable around me when I do that. Some people have asked me if I worry about not coming across as genuine. That has never been an issue in my experience. When I can make people feel comfortable, they are usually not wondering if I am sincere.

During an interview, you want to get people to like you so that they trust and confide in you by telling you the truth. I tell my students that people will only tell you the truth if they *want* to tell you the truth. They have to be motivated. Would you want to confide in an interviewer if they did not respect you, like you, and make you feel good? Probably not.

I smile a lot when I teach. When I see students in the room smiling back at me, it is usually because their mirror neurons were activated. Most of the time they are not smiling because they are happy, but because they are mirroring what they are observing. Scientists state that the same part of the brain is activated whether you feel an emotion or observe one. Thus, when you smile from reflection, you can feel happy.

I recently received my certificate in the Psychology of Leadership from Cornell University. In one of the classes, the professor discussed the impact of emotional contagion. As the term suggests, emotions can be contagious at an unconscious level. Have you ever been around someone who made you feel happy, sad, or angry, yet you didn't feel that way before interacting with them? You may have caught their emotion. Understanding this sensation and the impact our emotions can have during an interview is fundamental. If you are calm and relaxed, others around you will feel calm and relaxed. If your POI appears to be nervous and anxious (they are breathing rapidly, blinking their eyes more frequently, sweating, or exhibiting other physiological signs of stress), you need to calm them by being calm. If you feel nervous and anxious yourself and display that through your body language, your POI may start to feel nervous and anxious. If you are open with your body language, they will be open with their body language. And if you exude confidence and stay emotionally controlled, others will remain emotionally controlled. The science of mirror neurons is a great tool to use during any disagreement or conflict.

Before I move on to the third rapport method, I will share something interesting about mirror neurons. They are responsible for us yawning when we see someone else yawn. The next time you enter a space occupied by people, yawn, then scan the room to see who yawned after you. If someone yawns, it probably means they were watching you because yawns are contagious. So, if you want to know if you are the center of someone's attention, find out: yawn.

CHANGE YOUR LANGUAGE

The third method to connect with people involves how we speak. Believe it or not, the words we use can predict an unpleasant outcome during an interview. Some words carry a negative and accusatory tone to them, even if we do not mean for that tone to be present. We want to sound positive and nonaccusatory when we speak to others.

Positive language focuses on what can be done or what is being done, whereas negative language focuses on what cannot be done or what is not being done. Positive language sounds polite, respectful, and helpful. Most important, it does not put people on the defensive. When you use positive language, you often have a positive outcome.

The same goes for nonaccusatory language. When your words are nonaccusatory, your communication will be respectful, and your relationships will strengthen. Accusatory language has an undertone of blame. If you are accusatory, it will only cause people to be defensive and possibly aggressive. Here are some examples of accusatory language and how you can change it to nonaccusatory language:

- Instead of saying, "You're angry," you would want to ask, "How do you feel right now?" You would not want to say, "It appears I've angered you," or ask, "Have I made you angry?" because you are still assigning that person an emotion, and unless you are a mind reader, you can't do that. So ask them how they feel, and by doing so, you express empathy and keep them in a dialogue.
- Instead of saying, "You misinterpreted what I said," say, "Perhaps I could have been clearer with what I said." This way, it sounds like you're the one taking the blame for the miscommunication.
- If you think someone is lying to you, you wouldn't want to say, "You're lying!" The person you just accused of lying is most likely going to respond with, "No, I am not," even if they are. Instead, say, "It appears to me that there is more to the story," or, "I may be wrong, but it appears there is something else you want to tell me." You wouldn't want to say, "I may be wrong, but

it doesn't appear to me that you told me everything." Using "doesn't" turns that sentence into negative language.

- Instead of saying, "I know you left out details of where you were last night," say, "It seems to me that you want to share some more details about where you were last night." This way, you are using an embedded command while being non-accusatory. The embedded command is "you want to share." I once met with a senior member of an organization to sell a course on elicitation. I wanted this company as a client, so during my presentation, I used an embedded command. I told him, "When you decide now to purchase this training for your two hundred sales employees, you will see a significant increase in your revenue this quarter as a result of this training." He sat there, looking me in the eye with his hand to his chin (a power pose), listening intently. A day later, after our in-person meeting, he called me to ask me about my availability for the next three months. My embedded command to "decide now" worked! (Unfortunately, a week later, he left the company and I was left high and dry.)

Consider the words you choose to use in your communication carefully. I bet, even now, after reading these few examples on how to change your language, you may be thinking that you use negative and accusatory language unwittingly, and you may have been unaware of the consequences. The effects of changing your language to be positive and nonaccusatory can be life-changing. And it is so easy to do. Just practice it and retrain your brain! In the activity at the end of this chapter, I give you ten more examples to keep practicing. The answers are at the end of this book in Appendix C.

ASSIGN A POSITIVE TRAIT

After I have established common ground and the POI has warmed up to me, I will assign a positive trait to them as an effort to get them to open up, be honest, and tell me the truth. I use this technique when I feel that either the POI has lied to me or is withholding critical information. This method is also referred to as *"priming"* a person to be truthful and honest. Priming is a technique whereby exposure to one incentive influences a behavioral response without conscious intention. It occurs below the surface of conscious thought and thus can influence human behavior intuitively. To use this technique, you assign someone a trait that instinctively encourages them to act and behave in a particular manner. For example, assign traits such as honesty and integrity to persuade the other person to be honest and have integrity. This tactic works well because, inherently, people want to be truthful and honest, and they want to live up to what you say they are. As they listen to what you say unconsciously, the positive traits will affect their behavior. Here are some examples I have used with great success:

- "I may not like what you did, but I admire your honesty about it."
- "I've heard you have a reputation for being a guy people can trust, and I know I can trust you."

I know it may sound incredulous, but it works. When I feel the person I am interviewing is on the verge of telling the truth, I assign a positive trait to push them over the edge and spill the beans. Here are examples of positive traits I assign to people I believe are lying to me:

- "I know you are an honest person, even considering what you did; you're honest with yourself as to why you did it."
- "You have respect, and I know you respect yourself and me."

- "You are brave; you don't shy away from things that may be uncomfortable to talk about."
- "You believe in what is right, and you do what is right. I know that you know telling the truth is the right thing to do."
- "You're human, and humans make mistakes, even if our mistakes feel right at the time we make them. But as humans, we are accountable for everything we do, even our mistakes. I know you are a person who takes accountability for your actions. You're not a coward."

Although it may sound trite and far-fetched, this technique has proven successful in my decades of interviewing. I invite you to try it out. Remember, be sincere. Like flattery, a little goes a long way. If you oversell it, you will sound insincere, and you will lose the impact. Worse, it could result in a negative impact.

ASK FOR HELP

A former colleague of mine once told me, "Lena, the only reason why we help other people is because it makes us feel good." I'm not arguing that point, but I will tell you, when I can help others, it does make me feel good, so why wouldn't someone who has helped me feel good? When I ask my interviewee to "Help me understand," "Help me by being up front with me," or ask, "Can you help me?" they seem to be more amiable to offering up information. It is a simple request, and most people will not decline it. You can even use this at home on your children. Ask them to help you clean up the kitchen after dinner instead of stating they have to (even if they do!). You may even find they do a better job at cleaning the dishes.

I gave a keynote to a group of entrepreneurs. Afterward, one of the audience members came up to me and asked how he could inspire his employees to be more aware. I asked him what specifically was concerning him, and he said, "I just want them to pick up something on the floor if they see it! I want them to notice that the tables need to be washed." I said it might be an awareness issue, but I believed it was more of a motivational issue. I told him to start by asking his employees to help him instead of telling them what to do. And then, we could work on how to best connect with them and motivate them to take more initiative.

If you ask me what the single best technique is to use, out of all of the tools in your toolbox, it is rapport. You can persuade an uncooperative person to cooperate. In the next chapter, I will discuss how to find out personal drivers, motivations, and needs.

• • •

"Before you judge, make sure you're perfect."

—ANONYMOUS

ACTIVITY

Change negative language to positive and accusatory to nonaccusatory. The answers are in Appendix C.

1. "You're being rude."

2. "You can't treat me like that."

3. "You're going to miss the deadline."

4. "You aren't leaving until I have that report."

5. "You never hear anything I say."

(continues)

6. "You could care less about what I think."

7. "Don't tell me that you've changed."

8. "Don't raise your voice to me."

9. "You misinterpreted what I said."

10. "Why are you so angry?"

4

UNDERSTANDING PERSONAL DRIVERS, MOTIVATORS, AND NEEDS

N THE LAST chapter, we focused on connecting with people on a profound level to encourage trust and cooperation. While doing this, we must also be resilient when building rapport with people and handling emotions, both yours and theirs, so that we can bounce back after an uncomfortable or difficult situation. If your first attempt at establishing common ground backfires, be patient and try again. Remember, if you get frustrated with yourself, you may become annoyed with the POI. In turn, because of mirror neurons and emotional contagion, they may end up feeling your frustration and becoming agitated with you. Remain calm, practice emotional intelligence, and do not forget that humans need human interaction.

In this chapter, we are going to dig a little deeper into human behavior by examining ways to discover an individual's motivations. Motivations can be functional and psychological. Examples of functional motivators are job security, money, family obligations, materialistic items, and basic survival needs such as food, water, clothing,

44

medicine, safety, and shelter. Examples of psychological motivators include guilt and shame, reputation, credibility, role in society or the family, status, ego, and even love and belonging. When you can find out what will motivate a person to be honest, you can work that to your advantage and sway them to the truth. However, a person's motivator usually comes with an attached need. For example, if the motivation is safety, the person may want a new jail cell to protect them from certain prisoners. If the motivation is to rid the burden of guilt, the person may want to talk to someone who makes them feel safe. If the motivation is anonymity for telling the truth, the person's need may be protection from others.

My Strategic Law Enforcement Interviewing Course (SLIC) is focused on my nonaccusatory rapport-based techniques to gain full cooperation and information that goes beyond just a confession. I train officers to shift their mindset off of just going for a confession and on to fully exploiting every last detail of the event. I also train interviewers to be patient, especially when it comes to getting the POI near the breaking point: when they decide either to keep lying or to tell the truth. It is the most sensitive and crucial part of an interview. Any wrong move can persuade the POI to retreat. You can always tell when the breaking point is happening. The visual body language cues include the POI dropping their head, avoiding eye contact, and slumping with their shoulders curled inward. They appear to shrink and ball up. At this point, they are under severe emotional and mental stress. The body is closing up to be able to process it. Approach the POI carefully and create a safe, comfortable environment for them to break and tell you the truth. Do not judge, blame, or accuse them of anything. What you should do is empathize with them by saying something along the lines of, "I know you are processing a lot of information," then assign a positive trait, "but I know in the end you will have the courage to open up," and then the most important thing you can do is to enjoy the silence. Do not talk. Let the POI be the first to break the silence. If you keep talking, they won't need to. Now, if five minutes goes by and they are still silent, repeat my method: 1) Say an empathy statement; 2) Assign a positive trait; 3) Be silent.

WHAT DRIVES PEOPLE'S BEHAVIOR

Sometimes people will decide to lie to you because they are angry with you, and they perceive their anger as hatred toward you. Sometimes people will decide to lie to you because of the perceived fear of telling the truth and the consequences that come along with it. Other times they will lie to you because of an ideological reason. They may perceive that you do not share their values or their morality. Others may resist telling you the truth due to social factors and the perception of negative relationships (us vs. them, good vs. evil) or the belief that if they tell you the truth their affiliates will outcast them.

As an interviewer, you must know the driving forces behind why a POI may choose to be dishonest.

INWARD OR OUTWARD FOCUSED

Another factor that can drive behavior is whether or not a person is inward or outward focused. If someone is inward focused (IF), they are concerned with themselves and their well-being on a physical, emotional, and social level. They are also concerned with how others perceive them. If people listen to their inner voice, they may look at situations subjectively, considering new experiences through the lens of their personal feelings and opinions. Simply put, when our focus is inward, we care about how things affect us.

When someone is outward focused (OF), they are more concerned with how their actions affect others and less concerned with how they come across to others. OF people tend to look at situations objectively without any personal feelings or opinions attached. They are more concerned with how their actions can make others feel.

Knowing if someone is IF or OF can help you discover their motivations and needs, build rapport, and assign positive traits. For instance, if the person you are interviewing is an IF, they will fear telling the truth because of guilt, loss of credibility, or degradation of social status. If you are interviewing an OF and trying to get them to be honest, they may fear telling the truth because it could create enemies or put other people in compromising situations. It will be difficult to persuade an OF to rat out their friends. But you could easily influence an IF to dime out their buddies if they could benefit. Or say you try to play the guilt card on an OF person. It might not work because guilt is an inward emotion. Instead, you would have to introduce shame, which is an emotion based on external factors.

One word can make all the difference in whether you can convince someone to tell the truth. When I was interrogating Middle Eastern detainees in Camp Delta after 9/11, I tried to guilt them into telling me the information I needed such as locations of training camps, who was financing them, and when the next attack was going to happen. My attempt at making them feel guilty for lying had no effect. I thought they would feel guilty for lying to me because I was treating them with respect, giving them incentives, and trying to make them more comfortable. But then my interpreter gave me a cultural lesson. He told me that the detainees didn't resonate with the emotion of guilt. In their culture, they associate with the feeling of shame because they are outward focused and live in collective societies that are concerned with the group and its interconnections. They are mindful of everything they do because their actions affect the group. Americans live in individualistic societies that are concerned with the needs of the individual over the needs of the group. In these societies, you can use guilt as a tactic to influence someone to be honest.

LADDERING

When trying to discover drivers, motivations, and needs, you must
understand who this person is on a cultural and behavioral level.
Knowing their personality preference, change style preference (how
they handle change), decision-making style preference, communication style preference, and whether or not they are IF or OF can make
or break your negotiation or whether or not you get the truth.

Try to put yourself in the other person's circumstances by asking
what the value is of telling the truth or confessing to a crime. If you
were them, why would you want to tell the truth? If you can't answer
that question, you have to find out. An easy way to do that is to use an
interviewing technique called "laddering." Thomas J. Reynolds and
Jonathan Gutman, who coauthored "Laddering Theory, Method,
Analysis, and Interpretation," developed and introduced the laddering theory in 1988. Many businesses use laddering, in particular market researchers, to identify what drives people to purchase certain
products or services. Laddering looks for meaningful associations
people have to a product or service that influences whether or not
they will purchase it. Reynolds and Gutman state that when you can
understand the value a product has for a person or group of people,
you can market that product to fit those values and sell the product.
Laddering helps us to understand what behaviors influence a person's
decision-making process; in sales, this is specifically what will motivate a person to make the decision to purchase something.

As an interrogator, I used laddering to find out what would motivate a detainee to tell the truth. It worked so well that I now teach
laddering in my strategic interviewing classes. The technique is simple. It requires the interviewer to ask a series of probing questions,
interrogative questions beginning with "how" and "why," to determine a person's motivations. There is nothing mysterious or clandes-
tine about it. Yet, if done effectively, laddering can yield a ton of
valuable information.

Why is it called "laddering"? Because the technique aims to get to a higher level of knowledge. Imagine climbing up a ladder. You have to successfully reach each rung before you can get to the next higher rung. The higher you go, the harder it may be to reach the next rung. When trying to find out a person's motivations, for their purchase choice or, in my world, to tell the truth, you essentially climb up a ladder through conversation levels. You start off by talking about non-pertinent, rapport-based topics, then you progress to the more relevant topics that require the person to share more sensitive or personal information.

In the world of marketing, every product or service has attributes, according to Reynolds and Gutman. But the attributes alone don't sell the product; it's the value of the attributes that persuades people to buy it. Market researchers want to know why consumers value certain product attributes over others. If they can find that out, then they can sell the product based on those values. For example, if a person is looking to buy a car, they will look at the car's aesthetic appeal, gas mileage, safety features, and trade-in value. But the buyer may be considering another attribute that didn't occur to the salesperson: room for man's best friend. If the car can fit two people but it doesn't have room for a large dog, the man may feel he has no room for his best friend and may not buy the car. Market researchers want to know if a car will be more appealing to a consumer because it has good gas mileage or because it has room for a dog. Sometimes the value is measured individually, and sometimes demographically.

You have probably heard of Maslow's Hierarchy of Needs. Abraham Maslow, an American psychologist, developed a theory for human motivation. He believed people are motivated by a set of needs, not just rewards and desires, which he illustrated in a five-stage model in the shape of a pyramid. The essence of his theory was that humans have fundamental needs that progress up the pyramid, or ladder, to more complex needs, finally reaching self-actualization, which to Maslow meant total self-fulfillment. A person's needs can change, however, over time. While they may have filled a middle-of-the-pyramid need to be accepted and loved, they may have just lost a basic need for shelter. For example, a married couple divorce and the wife gets the house in the settlement. The husband, although perhaps loved by his family and children still, now has no shelter, which is a basic need.

I use a hierarchy of needs when trying to find out what will motivate a person to stop lying. I like to think of a person's motivation being affected by two factors: functional needs and emotional needs. As an interviewer, I am always trying to find the truth. To do so, I must know not only a person's motivations for telling the truth but also their needs that I have to address once they tell me the truth. Is it a functional need such as providing safety from others, or is it an emotional need such as being admired by peers? As you can imagine, both laddering and Maslow's Hierarchy of Needs are two critical tools for any type of interviewer.

I believe laddering has great value in the field of interviewing and interrogation, not just market research. I train many individuals from homicide detectives to private sector personnel investigating white-collar crimes, and I tell all of them, if you can't find out the motivation for a person to tell you the truth, they won't.

So how do we use the laddering technique? Laddering requires probing questions, which ask "how" and "why." As a former interrogator, I will tell you "why" questions can come across as aggressive and accusatory. They can put people on the defensive. So, I sprinkle "why" questions in with my other interrogative questions to deter a defensive posture.

Probing questions sound like this: "Why is that important/unimportant to you?" "How do you feel about that?" "How does that make you feel?" "Why do you think that?" They can get to the heart of the matter. However, you do not want to rapid-fire a list of probing questions off to someone because you will come across as accusatory. Your tone and rate of speech can also put a person on the defensive.

You should sound calm but confident. Be sure you have rapport first. Use positive and nonaccusatory language, or this technique may shut a person down.

Laddering can create a safe environment for people to confess because the questions you are asking are nonaccusatory and without judgment. Have patience and ask your questions sincerely and calmly. For laddering to work, however, you must ask intelligent questions. You have to listen to the words the interviewee says to formulate practical probing questions. By embedding the POI's language into your questions, it lets the person know you are paying attention to them. When the person hears their words repeated, it can emphasize their importance at an unconscious level.

When interviewing or negotiating, ask yourself, "Why will the POI tell me the truth?" If you can't answer that question, you probably won't get the truth. Oftentimes, interviewers like to think they can answer that question for the interviewee. A common response I hear is, "He has to confess; we have evidence." What if the person denies the evidence? Then what? If you can unveil a person's motivations and needs, and address their needs, you will increase your success of getting the truth. A way to do that is to provide a value for people to speak openly and honestly by assigning a personal value for telling the truth. As mentioned earlier in this chapter, there are two types of values you can assign: functional and psychological. Say you have an employee who you know is misusing company assets. Examples of assigned functional values to help convince the employee to be honest during questioning would be focused on job security and reputation. You may want to say, "If you help us now, the company may have leniency on you and allow you to keep your position." Or, "Until we know what happened, people may not trust your work, and that may lead to the loss of contracts and the loss of your position." Or, "The company is putting a lot of effort into this investigation and you may lose your position just so the company can avoid the effort." Or, "The company considers you a risk now and may let you go."

Examples of assigned psychological values to help convince the employee to be honest during questioning would be focused on negative emotions such as guilt, worry, shame, loss of integrity, and perceptions of others. Regarding psychological values, you may say, "If you are not honest, many companies will stay clear of you." Or, "Being honest reduces the stress and anxiety of lying as well as the fear of the unknown." Or, "Being honest makes you a good person." Or, "People may have a negative perception of you, especially if they believe you gave this company a scandal." Or, "Your actions could cost the reputation of this company, which can result in loss of jobs for many people. Do you realize the long-reaching aftereffects of your actions on people?"

Do you remember an individual by the name of Barry Minkow? He is an American conman and convicted felon. When he was in high school, he started his own business called ZZZZ Best Carpet and Furniture Cleaning, which he later used as a front for one of the biggest Ponzi schemes in US history. He graduated from high school in 1985 and worked full-time for his carpet-cleaning and restoration business. In 1986, he took his company public and claimed to be worth millions. He even went on the *Oprah* show touting his fame and fortune when the reality was that ZZZZ Best was a massive investment fraud. His business collapsed in 1987, costing investors and lenders millions. The scheme was so notorious that even today it is commonly used as a case study in accounting fraud classes.

When he was caught, he first lied and said that members of an organized crime family forced him to turn his company into a Ponzi scheme. Later he admitted that it was all his own doing. At one point, he gloated about how he was able to pull off the Ponzi scheme and offered to work with the FBI to help investigate fraud. And even after he came clean, he went right back to scheming people out of money. His motivator was his ego. He wanted to be smarter and wealthier than everyone else. He probably felt good to be liked and trusted when he confessed and became a "good guy." But with an underlying need for what I call the "God complex," he thought he could get away with another scheme. Once a con, always a con—it's what motivates him and fills a psychological need. Knowing this about Barry gives you the angle to use if you had to interview him. Barry is probably not going to respond to a pride and ego down approach that would make him feel guilty for misleading people. He would likely respond to a pride and ego up approach: "How brilliant you were to be able to mislead people!"

When you know what motivates someone and drives their thoughts and behaviors, you have leverage you can use to get them to open up to you. By being calm and patient, using laddering, and listening with awareness, you can discover a person's motivations and get them to tell the truth. Remember, people will only tell the truth if they *want* to tell the truth. They need to feel safe, and they need to trust you. Create a safe environment and gain their trust by being human, respectful, and authoritative. Listen, probe, and, finally, address their concerns and needs.

THE MOTIVATION EQUATION

To wrap up our conversation on understanding personal drivers, motivators, and needs, I am going to share the Motivation Equation with you.

Before I do, I want to encourage you to get in the practice of scripting your conversations before you have them, so you increase your chances of success. When you script your conversations, use the Motivation Equation to help you meet your objective(s). In most cases your objective is a *want* that will require the other person to *give*. What will persuade them to *want to give*? Their motivation for doing what it is you want them to do. That motivation will often come with servicing a need. To simplify this equation, look at it this way:

Their MOTIVATION + their NEED = your WANT

Or, if you flip the equation around, your *want* requires their *motivation*, which comes with a *need*. If you use this equation when planning your interview or negotiation strategies, you will be more successful in persuading and influencing others to give you what you want.

• • •

"The key to success is to focus on the goals, not obstacles."

—UNKNOWN

ACTIVITY: LADDERING

In the following three scenarios, come up with at least five probing questions you would ask to find out the POI's motivations. In Appendix C, you will find example questions for each scenario.

SCENARIO 1
POI is a seventeen-year-old girl who is being interviewed by the principal of her school about marijuana that fell out of her bag during class. Her mother is sitting beside her. The girl claims she has no idea how the marijuana got in her bag. You think she is lying. What probing questions could you ask her? Your objective is to find out her motivation and need in order to get her to tell the truth.

SCENARIO 2
You are an executive recruiter, and your potential job candidate will not answer your calls or return them. It has been one week since they said they were going to talk to their

(continues)

boss about terminating their employment so that you can place them in your client's company. They finally answer your call and apologize for not being able to call you back because they got busy, they were sick, and their car died. You don't believe them. What probing questions can you ask to find out why they were ghosting you? Your objective is to find out their motivation and need in order to get them to terminate their job and join the new company. Your objective is to have this person be excited to pay your asking price and join as a new client.

SCENARIO 3

You are an entrepreneur, and your goal this year is to grow your clients and your income significantly. You have been networking and marketing your program on social media. A potential client contacts you and wants to know how much you charge for one-on-one coaching services. You tell your price. They scoff and try to negotiate your price with you, but it is non-negotiable. What probing questions can you ask this person to find out why they do not want to pay your asking price? Your objective is to have this person be excited to pay your asking price and join as a new client.

5

MASTER YOUR QUESTIONING TECHNIQUES

S INCE THE TIME you could speak, you have been asking questions. And when you started speaking, your questions were simple, clear, and concise. You knew what you wanted, so you asked for it without being wordy or ambiguous. A friend and colleague of mine, James Pyle, author of *Find Out Anything from Anyone, Anytime*, used to say that we all started as natural-born questioners. Somewhere along the way, however, our questioning tactics changed. As adults, we are more conscious of how others perceive our questions. To avoid sounding too direct, we soften the blow of sensitive questions by making them wordier. Sometimes, intentionally or unintentionally, we end up concealing our question within a conversation. By the time we finish speaking, it's hard to identify the question. If our question is not clear to the listener, how can we expect them to answer it? We cannot expect an interviewee to answer questions that are a confusing run-on of words. Even if we intended to sound more agreeable and empathetic because the question we wanted to ask was delicate, the result could be more damaging than if we had just come out and asked directly.

Sometimes we expect the other person to *get* what we are asking. Even as adults, I bet there have been some conversations where you have said, "Oh, come on, you know what I mean!" If we want to be effective communicators, we cannot expect people to interpret what we are trying to ask. It's not their responsibility. Why would you want to do that? As Jim Pyle says, we have to go back in time and revert to asking questions like we did when we were kids. "When is my birthday?" "How many presents will I get?" "What kind of cake are you getting me?" Clear, concise, interrogative questions that are direct and to the point. When you can perfect how you ask a question, you can control a conversation, defuse aggression, win a high-stakes negotiation, and, of course, get information.

This chapter will retrain your brain to ask good questions while sounding respectful and maintaining rapport. This fundamental skill will give you the courage and confidence you need in your interview. All you have to do is think about what you want to know and ask for it! At the end of this chapter, you will find two activities to hone your questioning skills. The first will ask you to change ineffective questions to effective questions. This activity helps break our bad habits of asking poorly phrased questions. The second will ask you to develop ten specific interrogative questions about a particular subject while timing yourself. This activity helps work out the brain. The faster your mind can formulate effective questions, the quicker you can think of them in an interview when you need them.

An interview is only as good as the interviewer, and the most critical skill of an interviewer is how they ask questions. You will learn types of questions to use and which ones to avoid, how to question objectively vs. subjectively, and how to use questioning techniques specifically designed to get to the truth. Finally, you will learn what I call my "4 Lie Exposing Questions" to determine whether or not someone is lying to you. I use them as my "gut check" questions because truth-tellers tend to answer these four questions one way, and liars tend to answer them another. If someone isn't telling the truth, you will know what to say and how to say it to avoid sounding accusatory. If the POI senses any hint of accusation in your voice, you could unwittingly lead them to take a defensive posture, or worse, shut down completely.

QUESTION OBJECTIVELY

To question objectively means to avoid creating impressions that you have taken sides or that you do or do not believe the POI is truthful. When formulating your questions, do so without making assumptions. For example, do not assume the answer, emotion or reaction, information, or even deception. Assumptions may cause you to ask biased questions and can sway the responses you receive. My rule is that if I don't know something, I ask for it. By asking objective questions, you will get unbiased and impartial information in return.

The proper way to devise your questions is to take out any unnecessary words. Keep your questions to nouns and verbs, and avoid adjectives, adverbs, and overly descriptive words. For instance, say you ask your business partner, "Why did you speak to the client in yesterday's meeting that way?" Asking "why" makes the question sound accusatory, and "that way" is vague. To ask that same question without placing blame, change your words. "How did you speak to the client in yesterday's meeting?" It is objective, unbiased, and nonaccusatory.

Another example is if you ask your child, "Did you take out the trash as I asked you to?" First, it is a yes-or-no question, making it easy for the child to lie if they haven't taken out the trash. Second, that question is too wordy and accusatory and will only invite a child's defensive posture. Instead, you would want to ask, "When did you take out the trash today?" Now you sound as though you are assuming they took out the trash and that you trusted them to do it. If they haven't done their chore, they may feel a bit of guilt because you were non-accusatory, and instead of lashing out defensively, you may get an honest answer, or they may say, "Sorry, I'll do it now." If you ask a suspect, "What were you thinking when you stole the car?" the suspect may feel you are patronizing them for what they have done, which may influence them to become defensive and close up. Instead, ask, "How did you feel when you stole the car?"

Words matter. All it takes is one word to make someone put their guard up and stop sharing information. You already learned how to change your language from accusatory to nonaccusatory and negative to positive. Now, consider every word you use in your questions because each has an impact. You want that impact to be a positive one.

TWO QUESTION TYPES

There are two types of questions, open-ended, also called interrogative questions; and closed-ended, commonly referred to as yes-or-no questions. An interrogative question starts with an interrogative: who, what, where, when, why, or how. It elicits a narrative response. Closed-ended questions usually begin with words such as did/do, are/is, could/would/should, and only invites a yes-or-no answer. If you ask poorly phrased questions, you will inevitably frustrate yourself and the person you are interviewing. If your questions are not straightforward, the interviewer might not respond in the manner you expect. If the POI's response to one of your questions is vague, you may assume they are trying to avoid answering when the reality is that your question was confusing. If you become irritated with the POI's answer, they may grow angry with you, and then the interviewer/interviewee relationship may suffer.

If you remember to begin your question with "who, what, where, when, why, and how," you will get information. And if your question is well formulated, you will get the information you seek. Because open-ended questions require a narrative response, you can encourage an uncooperative person to keep talking by asking them. You can also keep a talkative person focused on providing details on particular topics. Interrogative questions can assist a POI in remembering details they could not recall at first. Interrogative questions also allow a person to share as much information as they wish without feeling pressured, encouraging cooperation and rapport. Interrogative questions keep the conversation flowing and encourage the POI to feel safe while providing sensitive material.

Do not make your questions too wordy or confusing. Phrase them with one subject and one verb only. For example, ask, "What work have you been doing since your graduation?" instead of "What do you do for work these days since graduating, or did you decide not to work yet? I know you were thinking about taking a break before finding a full-time job." That last question is not even a question at all. It started as one but then became a long-winded and confusing narrative statement. When interrogators do not fully trust their interviewing skills, they tend to ask a good question, then follow up with fluff that cancels out the question and adds confusion. If you ask a question and realize it was ineffective, let it go. Do not try to cover it up with more words or rephrase it. Wait until they answer and then ask another question. For example, if you asked, "Do you know who took the money?" and realize that person could easily say "no" and lie, let it go, and then ask an interrogative question: "Who took the money?"

There is one purpose for a closed-ended question: when you want to verify and clarify something or check for deception. In fact, two of my four lie-exposing questions are yes-or-no questions. As I'll explain later, I use them as a gut check to ensure my interviewees are honest. Other than for this purpose, I refrain from asking closed-ended questions. For example, if you want to find out the name of someone's spouse and you are not sure if they are married, you wouldn't want to ask, "Are you married?" Simply ask, "What is your spouse's name?" If they are not married, they will tell you that, and if they are, they will tell you their spouse's name.

REPEAT AND CONTROL INTERROGATIVES

You can use interrogative questions to help validate the accuracy of the information the POI is giving you, especially if you do not have their full trust or cooperation. During the interview, you can and should ask two styles of interrogative questions: "repeat" and "control." A repeat interrogative is just what the name implies. It is a question you have previously asked that you ask again to verify the answer and ensure the POI is consistent. Is the information the same, or has it changed? If it is the same, the information may be truthful. If it is different, the POI may have lied. They could also be telling the truth but became confused or tuned you out for a moment and didn't hear your question. As the interviewer, you need to determine why there was a discrepancy in the information without automatically assuming the POI is lying. You will have to use your detecting deception skills, which we will discuss later on.

When asking repeat interrogatives, you can either phrase the question the same way or change the words so it appears as though it is a different question. For example, if I ask you, "What time did you leave work last night?" I can ask the same exact question a few minutes later, or better, I can change it slightly: "When you left work last night, what time was it?" I am listening to see if I get the same answer.

A control interrogative also allows you to check for the truthfulness of the POI and the accuracy of the information. Say you ask someone, "What time did you leave work last night?" and they answer, "Eight." You can check the truthfulness and accuracy of that answer by asking this control interrogative a few minutes later: "When you left work at 9:00 p.m., who was with you?" Control interrogatives purposely falsify a piece of known information to test the POI. If the POI corrects the false information, that is a sign they are truthful. If the POI does not correct the incorrect information, they could be lying. Again, do not jump the gun to assume deception. The

POI may not have been paying full attention to your question, or they may have gotten confused.

Using control interrogatives on known and verified information is a great technique to check for deception. But use them carefully and sparingly. Avoid being too specific because you may cause the POI concern, and you can tip your hand regarding the evidence you have and the information you don't have. If you use too many repeat and control questions, the POI may catch on and start to ask you why you keep asking the same question or why you are not taking better notes. Trust and rapport could be lost. I had this happen to me once while I was interrogating. I asked the detainee a repeat question, and even though I waited fifteen minutes to ask it again, the detainee was wise. He remembered I had asked the question before, and instead of answering the question again, he said something in Arabic. My interpreter translated what the detainee said: "You already asked me that. Are you not taking notes?" I had to think on my feet, and I responded with, "Yes, I am taking notes. I could not read my handwriting, so I had to ask you again." The detainee frowned, shrugged his shoulders, and answered the question again. Thankfully, the information was consistent.

I recently taught a three-day strategic interviewing class to state and federal law enforcement. I wrapped up the class with an activity called "hot-seat" exercises. Here's how it works: A student sits in a chair in front of the class and tells us two stories; one is a lie. Based on the training, the class has to determine which one is the lie. In this case, it was a US marshal who took the hot seat. He told the class two stories; one was truthful, and the other was a lie. I was 99 percent certain which one was his lie. To be 100 percent certain, I asked him a control question. His lie was about a skiing trip he took to Keystone, Colorado. Aside from not being able to give any details about skiing, or what he wore, and mislabeling the intermediate trail red, not blue, when I asked him, "When you were at Aspen, how many hours did you ski?" he said, "Pretty much all day." First, he didn't correct me after I purposely changed Keystone to Aspen; second, he gave me a squishy answer. To make sure he wasn't just tuning me out, or he didn't hear me say "Aspen," I asked another control question: "How many days did you stay at Aspen?" He answered, "About three." Now I knew he was lying! He didn't correct me again, and he used the liars' number three! Liars tend to use "three" when they are put on the spot and have to quantify information that is not true. Finally, I asked, flippantly, "Is there any reason why you didn't correct me when I said you were skiing at Aspen?" He just stared at me. I got him. In the debrief, he said he never heard me say "Aspen" because he was so nervous.

FOLLOW-UP

Another common mistake first-time or inexperienced interviewers make is neglecting to follow up on information provided by the POI by drilling down about a person, place, or thing until the interviewee has no more information to provide.

When drilling down, you may get stuck and unable to think of a follow-up question. If you hit a wall, as I refer to it, and are unsure what to follow up on, remember this guideline: define all nouns and describe all verbs. Every sentence has nouns and verbs, even the one I am writing right now. So, if you hit a wall, all you have to do is ask questions about the nouns and verbs you hear. This way, you leave no stone unturned.

Asking follow-up or drill-down interrogatives can buy you time to think about the relevant topics you need to exploit further. As you do this, you may hear new information leads; perhaps an avenue to new information that could solve a case. If the lead is important and time-sensitive, immediately ask questions about that information. If the lead is not that significant, make a note to go back and ask questions about it later if you have time. Also, do not tune out while the POI is speaking. If you do, you will miss an opportunity to identify new, previously unknown material. Our minds will inevitably wander. We must realize it and bring our attention back to the POI.

Here's what can happen if you do not remember to ask follow-up questions. Say you ask your partner, "Who went out with you last night?" and they tell you, "Chris." How do you know they only went out with Chris? To be sure, ask a follow-up question: "Who else went out with you last night?" If they answer with, "Oh, Jim and Jill met us too," then you will have received another positive response. Now you will have to dig for more information. So ask again, "Who else did you go out with last night?" "We saw Christine and Blake there, but we didn't necessarily go out with them." You still haven't received a negative response yet, so at the risk of sounding like a robot, you continue: "Who else went out with you last night?" Finally, you receive a negative response: "I didn't go out with anyone else." Now you can cease the follow-ups. If your partner said, "No one else was there," that is not the same as "I didn't go out with anyone else." We'll get more into that in chapter 12 when I teach you statement and word analysis.

Always remember, when you are drilling down on a topic, noun, or verb, make sure that, once you finish, you go back to your original line of questioning so that you do not leave any information unexploited. Cunning POIs who want to avoid answering your questions about an incriminating topic may try to control the conversation and take you down a rabbit hole that leads you nowhere. They may make up fictitious leads so that you stop asking about one topic and start asking about a new topic. People who have something to hide will try to guide your attention away from what they can't talk about. As the interviewer, you must identify when someone has purposely taken control of the interview and is giving you a smoke screen to disguise their true intentions.

QUESTIONS TO AVOID

I will share five examples of questions you should avoid because they will cause confusion and frustration and lead to false and incomplete information. The first, called a leading question, is phrased in such a way as to suggest the desired answer, thereby prompting incomplete or potentially invalid information. Leading questions are closed-ended and sometimes referred to as suggestive questions because they indicate what the answer should be. For example: "Are you afraid that if you give me the information, someone will harm you?" This question suggests that the interviewee is afraid to give information because someone will harm them. It also indicates that the interviewer knows this to be true. If you do not understand why the person is not talking, don't assume they are too scared to speak. If a POI tells you they are too scared to talk, do not assume what they fear. If they don't want to talk because they don't want to tell you the truth, you just gave them a way out. Because all an uncooperative person has to say as a response to that question is, "Yes, I'm not talking because I'm scared someone will harm me." A better question would be, "How do you feel about giving me information?" or, "What concerns do you have speaking with me?" Leading questions heavily influence the answer to the question being asked. It's as though the person asking the leading question is coercing the POI to agree with them. Leading questions provide a perfect opportunity for someone to get away with not being responsible or accountable for their actions.

In law enforcement, this has been a common technique to soften up the harshness of a crime or event so that a suspect or witness feels more comfortable talking about it. A typical scenario I hear regarding the use and sale of illegal substances is, "I get that you had to sell drugs to feed your family." Unless the POI tells you that is why they are selling drugs, you should never say this because you could be giving them a way out. You may never learn that they sell drugs because it's their business, and they like the cash.

Some lawyers like to use leading questions to bait and trap witnesses. A defense attorney tried to bait and trap me once while I was in GTMO, serving as a prosecution witness for one of the detainees I had interrogated. The prosecution team subpoenaed me to be a witness in the war tribunals that took place in 2007, around four years after I left GTMO. The military commissions were organized to charge the unlawful enemy combatants with war crimes. The detainee I had interrogated was charged with murdering a US military member, attempting to murder, conspiracy, and spying. During my first-ever cross-examination, the judge seemed to loom over me, and I remember being nervous on the witness stand. However, being an experienced interrogator, I knew all the techniques, tricks, and ruses one can use to trap people. A leading question is one of those tactics. The defense attorney asked me, "You are aware of my client's culture, right?" Of course, I was, and knowing that this was a leading question, I hesitated before saying "yes" to see if the lawyer could use my response against me. I decided he couldn't, so I answered. After all, it was a yes-or-no question. Then the defense attorney asked me, "Then isn't it true that you know being a female made my client uncomfortable because of his cultural background?" I almost laughed at the ridiculousness of this question. Especially when the detainee and I spent hours talking, playing games, and eating meals together during our interrogations. He had asked a yes-or-no question, but he wanted to lead me into a trap this time. If I answered "no," he could have come back and said, "Then you don't know my client's culture, and yet you call yourself a trained interrogator?" If I said, "yes," he could have come back and said, "Well, then you agree that you knew you made my client uncomfortable during your interrogations!" What could I do? I looked up at the judge and said, "Your Honor, I will not answer that question. It is a leading question, and the defense attorney is trying to trap me to look guilty." The judge was so angry that he slammed his gavel. There was a mild roar in the courtroom. The judge leaned down closer to my face and asked, "You have to answer the question! Why won't you answer it?" I calmly explained that I couldn't answer because the information would be biased and used against me. "Your Honor," I said, "I will gladly answer any question the defense attorney has if it is an interrogative question." After a few minutes of glaring at me, he slammed his gavel again, looked at the defense attorney, and said, "Change your question." The defense attorney's response was, "No further questions." Later that night, when the press released their stories to the world, I read one article that said, "Agent 11 [my code name] mentally sparred with the defense attorney and won." Do not ask leading questions.

The second question you should avoid using is called a negative question. Negative questions begin with a contraction: "Didn't," "Couldn't," "Wouldn't," "Shouldn't," "Wasn't," or "Weren't." Negative questions are confusing and will almost always require clarification. Here is an example: "Aren't you learning a lot from this chapter?" How do you answer that? If you respond with "yes," I don't know if you are telling me, "yes, I am," or, "yes, I'm not (aren't)." Negative questions waste time because you will have to ask another question to clarify the confusion. They will also frustrate you and the person you are questioning. A simple fix is to ask, "How much are you learning from this chapter?"

The third question to avoid is two questions in one, known as a compound question. Compound questions may create misunderstandings, confusion, and frustration both in the interviewer and the POI. For example, "Who were you with, and where did you go?" If the POI only answers one of the questions, the interviewer may wrongly assume the POI answered only one to avoid the other. Perhaps the POI only heard one part of the compound question or simply forgot to answer the other. The POI could think that you changed your mind about the first question and want them to answer the second question instead.

Compound questions are probably the most commonly used ineffective question type and thus the most damaging. They will compromise your ability to gain detailed information without causing frustration. But if you ask a compound question and the POI answers only one question, and then you forget to go back and ask the other question, you can lose your credibility. When you are interviewing uncooperative and aggressive people looking for every way to deceive you, it becomes a game of how many wins they can get. By being able to evade your question, the POI gains a victory. They may even think they have gained control of the interview or interrogation.

The fourth question you want to refrain from asking is known as a forced-choice question, which forces someone to make a choice, though the actual correct answer may not be one of the options you provided. These questions do not yield reliable, truthful information, and they can be accusatory. For example, "Would you rather decide now or later?" If the person doesn't want to decide, you force them into choosing now or later. Or say you ask someone, "Do you take the bus or drive to work?" What if the person gets a ride from a friend? If you ask someone, "Which leader do you think is best, a liked leader or a feared one?" What if it is neither? Notice that two out of three of these forced-choice questions are also closed-ended.

And finally, when you need detailed information, avoid asking vague questions. These may be appropriately phrased by starting with an interrogative, but they are still ineffective because of the lack of information they produce. If you ask a vague question, you get a vague answer. Asking vague questions when your goal is to obtain specific information will only force you to ask more follow-up questions to get more details, which could frustrate others and take much time. For example, if I want to find out the city you were born in, I will ask you, "What is the name of the city you were born in?" instead of asking you something vague like, "Where are you from?" Most of us understand what this question means and what the questioner expects our answer to be. But if you are interviewing someone who speaks a different language and using an interpreter, the answer may be unexpected. "Where are you from?" can mean "Where did you grow up?" "Where were you born?" or "Where do you live now?" People can interpret the question differently. So, ask for what you want! If you want to know the address of where a person lives now, that is what you ask. If you want to find out the name of the town or city they were born in, that is what you ask.

Asking vague questions also provides a way out of giving up details, especially if you are interviewing someone who doesn't want to give you those details. If you ask an uncooperative POI, "Where are you from?" they may answer, "The South." Is that truly what you wanted to know? When I feel a stranger is too pushy and forward with finding out information from me, I answer politely, but not with the answer they expect. When I am asked, "What do you do for a living?" I say I teach. If they ask, "What do you teach?" I tell them interpersonal communication skills. Then, usually, they become bored and move on. Protect yourself and your information. You wouldn't want a criminal to know your true name, a disgruntled employee to know your address, or a competitor to know your trade secrets. When asked a vague question, you can be polite and respectful while not giving up the information you know someone wants. Imagine attending a trade show with multiple competing vendors. One asks, "Who else have you talked to today regarding this product, and what did they offer?" You don't have to stammer, or nervously laugh it off, or refuse to respond. You can give them a vague answer. "They are not offering much. What are you offering?"

QUESTIONING TECHNIQUES TO HELP YOU GET THE TRUTH

Here are five techniques that can help you persuade someone to tell the whole truth:

1. *Ask nonpertinent questions.* This may be a properly phrased effective interrogative question, but it is an unimportant

question that has nothing to do with the relevant information you need to collect. Nonpertinent questions are great to use when building and reinforcing rapport with the POI. Nonpertinent questions focus on hobbies, the weather, favorite food and sports, family, and friends. The POI will not hesitate to answer these questions. They can decrease stress that may have arisen during the interview, and disguise the information you are after. You can ask nonpertinent questions to buy you time to get organized, collect your thoughts, analyze your notes, and think of your next pertinent questions. Nonpertinent questions are unexpected, and as such, they can break the POI's concentration. This can be valuable when a POI is lying and trying to remember the lie.

2. *Adopt a pause.* Take a moment before you begin speaking. By doing this, you can entice the POI to say more without having to ask for it. For example, when my POI answers a question, I sometimes do not immediately respond with another question. Instead, I keep eye contact and wait for a few seconds, not too long that the silence becomes awkward but long enough to see if they want to add additional information. I find that when I look at the POI in silence, not in a rude and accusatory way but in an inquisitive manner, the POI feels as though I know that they have more to say. Since people are usually uncomfortable with silence, especially if there is any worry or guilt about concealing information, they will usually start talking again. You cannot rush when using this technique; it requires patience. You are pausing to adjust the pacing of the question/answer cadence.

3. *Exploit with rapid fire.* Ask straightforward, simple interrogative questions in rapid succession. This technique is one of my favorites because it always catches people off guard. For the rapid-fire approach to be practical, you must be confident in your questioning abilities. Rapid-fire questioning is

the opposite of pausing and pacing. Ask a specific, clear, concise, interrogative question, and then wait for the answer. Based on the answer, ask another interrogative question within seconds of the POI responding. Keep this up for a few minutes. Sometimes I even cut the POI off mid-sentence (something we should not do, but this technique is the exception). I apologize for interrupting them, or I tell them I knew that information already, and follow up immediately with another question. Doing this keeps the POI off-balance and on guard. If they are trying to remember a rehearsed lie, it will be tough.

You want the person you are interviewing to feel comfortable and relaxed so that they are confident and clearheaded. However, this can have an adverse effect. If your POI is lying, they may remember their lie better because cortisol (a stress hormone released by our adrenal glands) has not impaired their cognitive ability. The presence of cortisol is not always a bad thing. In fact, according to *Psychology Today*, there are two kinds of stress: good (eustress) and bad (distress). Good stress is when the right amount of cortisol levels fuel your passion, will, and determination. However, too much cortisol release can interfere with their capacity to translate, store, and recall memory. When a person is in this state, they are not calm and may inadvertently leak information. It also impairs their ability to keep the details of their lie straight. Keeping a POI thinking on their feet will affect their ability to remember a rehearsed lie. If a POI can anticipate things during an interview, such as what you know and do not know, your next questions, your reactions, or what will happen to them, they may have an easier time lying to you because they will be more relaxed and comfortable.

I have gotten many people to accidentally provide truthful information or mix up the details of their lie by keeping them

off-balance and wondering what's coming next. If you suspect the POI is lying to you, do something to keep them
off-balance. Ask a nonpertinent or unanticipated question,
use the rapid-fire approach, or use the Columbo Approach.

4. *Use the "Columbo Approach."* When I was interrogating in
Camp Delta, I was assigned interpreters because I didn't
speak Arabic, Pashtu, Uighur, or Dari. After an interrogation,
my interpreter and I usually had to wait a few minutes for
the guards to come to the interrogation room to escort the
detainee back to their cell inside the camp. I am one to make
every second count, so I would continue to ask questions
while we waited for the guards. I never took notes, making
it seem more like a casual conversation than an interrogation. I began to notice how much more information I could
get in those few minutes when the detainee thought I was
finished with the "interrogation." It became common practice for me. As a result, my interpreters gave me the nickname "Columbo." The "Columbo Approach" is when you ask
questions that come across to the POI as though you have no
plan, no objectives, and no agenda. Sometimes I would pretend to be ignorant or simpleminded about important topics
in which I was actually well versed. I would act like I didn't
need to be "in-the-know," as if it didn't matter whether they
answered. It worked! The detainees would drop their guard.
They were relaxed because they knew they were going back
to their cell, and it was during this time I collected some of
my most sensitive intelligence.

This approach is effective because it falls right between
hypervigilance and absentmindedness. It suggests that, instead of judging the POI, you are seeking help from them to
understand their situation. When the POI thinks you are
through asking questions, you can throw in a few last-minute
questions that appear to be random afterthoughts.

72

Here is an example of how to use the Columbo Approach: If the POI says, "I can't remember what exactly happened that night," you could say, "Help me understand this: you can't remember what exactly happened that night, but you did an outstanding job of recalling the details of what you did the night before that night." And then pause to see what they say next. The Columbo Approach doesn't ask questions; it makes statements intended to have an impact. I would usually start by saying something like this: "You know, I still can't believe you were able to coordinate that well without cell phones." Anything that related to the interrogation but that appeared unrelated. They bit every time.

Columbo also liked to switch up the topics unexpectedly to make it appear as though he had no clue what he was saying. When you do this, the POI may think you've confused yourself and forgot to ask them more questions about the previous topic. They may assume you are incompetent, let their guard down, and confuse the details of their story. Then you present all the facts and details to show them their discrepancies, proving you were focused and in control the entire time. Appearing jumbled and confused, Columbo seemed to give the suspect the benefit of the doubt. The funny thing is he was brilliant and always knew when someone was guilty.

5. *Timeline.* Timelining is my go-to technique to catch lies and exploit every last bit of detail of a story. I like to say details are the death of a lie because if the POI fails to provide details, that could be an indicator of deception. On the other hand, if the POI does provide details, but they are lies, they will not be able to remember those fabricated details later during questioning, especially when you use this technique.

Did you know that liars cannot remember a lie backward? Liars do not practice telling their lie in reverse. Timelining their story, writing down key events they tell you on a timeline, either horizontally or vertically, allows you to see their story in reverse. So if you ask them to tell you about their story again, but this time going backward from point B to A, they will not be able to do it. They will reach what we call cognitive overload.

If you use this technique, you have to be a good listener and notetaker. Usually, if a POI is lying, they will tell you just enough information to make it appear as though they are cooperating. But as interviewers, we want and need details. Timelining will help you collect all of the details of any story. When you write their story on paper in a timeline format, you can view it as a series of events in chronological order, which will allow you to see the gaps of information between each "tick" on the timeline. I will show you a real-world example from Larry King's live interview with Patsy and John Ramsey in 2000, four years after their daughter, JonBenet, was found murdered in their home. Although Larry King did not timeline, you can right now. I transcribed part of the conversation, but I encourage you to watch the interview here: https://www.youtube.com/watch?v=HhfgP_vkO1c.

Here is a portion of that interview that I transcribed. (Larry King = LK; John Ramsey = JR; Patsy Ramsey = PR.)

LK: "What happened that night? What's the first thing you remember, Patsy?"

PR: "The first thing I remember is . . . waking up, getting dressed hurriedly, going downstairs, and, uh, putting a few things together to pack to take on the plane . . ."

(On my timeline, I wrote: 1st tick mark—waking up; 2nd tick mark—getting dressed; 3rd tick mark—going downstairs to pack.)

LK: "This is about what time?"

PR: "It's early morning, before daylight."

LK: [to John Ramsey] "You're up?"

JR and PR: "Mm-hmm."

LK: "Then what happened?"

PR: "Then I, I [stutter] go down the spiral staircase [makes a spiral motion with her hands] and . . . there, on one of the rungs of the stair is a 3-page ransom note."

(On my timeline, I write: 4th tick mark—go down "spiral" staircase; 5th tick mark—finds 3-page ransom note on the stair.)

LK: "And no one has entered the house, door isn't open, you read the note."

PR: [smiling] "I don't know that . . ."

LK: "What did you do?"

PR: [still smiling] "Well, I hardly even read it, you know, and didn't take long to understand . . . what . . . was happening, and I ran back upstairs and pushed open her bedroom door, and she was gone."

(On my timeline, I write: 6th tick mark—hardly read the note; 7th tick mark—ran back upstairs; 8th tick mark—pushed open her door & she was gone.)

You may have noticed that there is a discrepancy in Patsy's story that revealed itself on the timeline. She went downstairs twice. Admittedly, I do not know the floor plan of their home. There could have been two sets of stairs, and she went down a different staircase earlier. Or it could be that she lied and got confused. Either way, she never told us she went back upstairs before "going down the spiral staircase." If I were interviewing her, I would have asked her specific questions to include the exact times of the events that morning. Even if she gave approximation times, you could still use them to uncover discrepancies. Another problem I have with Patsy's story is that she switches from present tense to past tense after finding the ransom note. This is a glaring indicator of deception.

Timelining also allows you to ask what happened between each tick mark to get more details of the story. You can use these details to help you check for truthfulness and accuracy with your repeat and control questions.

MY FOUR LIE-EXPOSING QUESTIONS

Typically, liars will respond one way and truth-tellers another. So the responses to these four questions usually can tell me if someone is being truthful or not.

1. *How did that make you feel?* Liars forget to attach feelings and emotions to their lies. When asked how they felt about something they lied about, a person will have to pause to think of how they should have felt. They will usually hesitate when answering, sound insincere, or respond with voice inflection as if they were asking a question.

2. *Why should I believe you?* A truthful person will usually say, "Because I'm telling you the truth." A liar will usually say something along the lines of, "Because I'm not lying." Truth-tellers tend to speak in the positive, and liars tend to speak in the negative and take a defensive attitude: "I'm not" vs. "I am." That statement is not 100 percent accurate; nothing is when it comes to detecting deception. But when used in

combination with my other lie-exposing questions, it can be correct.

3. *What do you think should happen to the person who did this?* If you ask a person you suspect of doing something this question, and they show signs of leniency in their answer, they are usually guilty of something. For example, say you ask your colleague, "What do you think should happen to the person who ratted out Mary for missing the deadline?" And say your colleague responds, "Well, perhaps they didn't know it would get her fired. They may not have said anything." Your colleague has guilty knowledge. A truthful person who does not know who did the activity will usually say, "They should be punished and held accountable." An innocent person wants to see the guilty person punished for the crime, plain and simple.

Remember Tom Brady, the former New England Patriots quarterback, and Deflategate (a play on words referring to the infamous Watergate scandal in Washington, DC, which led to President Nixon resigning)? Deflategate had nothing to do with Washington politics, but it rocked the NFL. The short story was that, in the 2014 AFC Championship Game, it was alleged that Brady ordered someone to deflate the footballs to give him an advantage on the field for a game against the Indianapolis Colts. During a press conference, a reporter asked him, "Is it important for you and the legacy of this team that someone is held accountable?" Brady's response was this: "Well that's for, you know I'm not the one that imposes, you know, those type of, you know accountability, it's, you know, discipline, all that, that's, you know, not really my job, so . . ." He may not have deflated the footballs himself. Still, he showed verbal indicators of deception such as filler words, setup words, and assuming language, which you will read about in chapter 12.

4. *Are you a liar? / Did you lie to me?* This is a yes-or-no question. If they do not answer, "no," then you have a problem! If that person is lying, they are aware of it, so you will see and hear deceptive indicators. Your job is to find out what they lied about or cheated on. I will usually abide by the three-strikes-you're-out rule. I will ask you three yes-or-no questions, and if you still cannot definitively answer "no," you most likely are trying to deceive me. And if you are incongruent with your body language, so you say "no" with your words, but your head is nodding yes, then you are probably not being truthful.

Lastly, do not jeopardize the integrity of your questions and questioning techniques. When I first deployed to Guantanamo Bay to interrogate detainees at Camp Delta, I hesitated to ask direct questions because I thought the detainees would think I was harsh and unpleasant. I was so concerned about building rapport and gaining cooperation that my objective suffered. My questions were terrible, and I got nowhere. I obtained no actionable intelligence information. I realized I was failing in my assignment, so I changed gears. In my next interrogation, I asked questions as I was taught to do, and finally, I acquired pertinent information and answered intelligence requirements. You can be friendly and respectful while asking straightforward, concise, direct questions. You have to be.

During those first couple of weeks as an interrogator at Camp Delta, I discovered interrogation was an art and a science. There is a process, and techniques to use, but you have to have finesse when using them. Tact, grace, diplomacy, and wit are critical skills for any successful interviewer. So, while stationed in GTMO, I began developing the nonaccusatory strategic interviewing technique that I still use today. I wanted to create a strategy to hone my ability to connect with the people I interrogated, first so that they would want to converse with me, and second, so they would want to tell me the truth. Because of its success, it has become the go-to interviewing training for law enforcement today.

After years of success and being able to "break" uncooperative POIs (breaking their will to resist telling the truth), I know that my technique can help any person who conducts interviews, formally or informally.

● ● ●

"Most people do not listen with the intent to understand;
they listen with the intent to reply."

—STEPHEN COVEY

ACTIVITY A

Change ineffective questions to effective questions. The answers are in Appendix C.

1. Are you mad?

2. Do you take the bus or drive to work in the morning?

3. Will you be arriving early?

4. Won't you ever stop complaining?

5. Do you prefer your mother's cooking or your grandmother's?

6. Were they upset with what happened?

7. Didn't you say she said "no" when you asked her?

8. Is she applying for jobs?

ACTIVITY B

Come up with ten questions in two minutes. This is a timed activity.

STEP 1

First, think of a person you do not know personally. It could be a celebrity, a political figure, or even someone at work you do not interact with often. Your goal is to find out more information about them by coming up with ten questions to ask them if you were face-to-face with them.

STEP 2

You have two minutes to come up with ten interrogative questions. Don't cheat! Set a timer for two minutes, and as quickly as you can, write ten questions on a piece of paper. Go!

STEP 3

How many interrogative questions were you able to come up with? If you wrote down questions that began with "Did you . . . Are they . . . Is your . . . ," those are yes-or-no, closed-ended questions. If you did write down closed-ended questions, try and change them to interrogative now.

When I do this activity in my classes, I rarely have anyone who comes up with ten questions. The majority of participants come up with four to six good, interrogative questions. However, after they have had the class, I do this same exercise again. And guess what? Most of the participants can now come up with seven to ten questions. In just a few hours, their questioning ability has improved. And so will yours. You just have to keep practicing.

(continues)

To keep practicing, do the same exercise again. If you want to challenge yourself, give yourself one minute to come up with ten interrogative questions. The more you exercise your brain, the faster you will formulate good questions during an interview when you need them.

You can try this with other topics such as sports, hobbies, or books. What ten questions would you ask a quarterback? An equestrian? An expert shooter? A professor? A business owner?

ACTIVITY WITH ANSWERS

Write ten specific interrogative questions you can ask an author within two minutes. Afterward, go to Appendix C to see my ten and compare them to yours.

6

DON'T TELL, ASK

NTERVIEWING IS NOT about getting a confession or an admission of guilt. It is about getting information that answers current, past, and future requirements while revealing motives and intent for current, past, and future events. That doesn't mean you won't get a confession or admission to guilt; what it means is that you will get much more beyond that. You may be wondering what more you would need from a suspect who admitted to committing murder. You are about to find out.

Some law enforcement interviewing practices use the "minimization" technique, where the interviewer downplays the crime or the accusation to make it appear less harsh than it is. This technique is supposed to offer suspects a way out of confessing to the actual crime by allowing them to admit to what appears to be a less severe one. My question is, why would any interviewer want to do that? Minimization allows a person a way out of telling the whole truth. In my opinion, minimization is just as ineffective and damaging as asking leading questions. I will explain why in this chapter. I will also give you an alternative technique to use, mine, which I call "Don't Tell, Ask," to get the entire unbiased truth and not a confession to a less serious crime.

First, let's look at an example of minimization. Say you are interviewing a suspect who murdered her boyfriend, but she won't fess up. You decide to use minimization to get her to confess. So you tell her, "Maybe you did it in self-defense." If she intentionally killed her boyfriend and thinks she can get away with lying, then this is an excellent alternative to admitting she killed him in cold blood because she went into a jealous rage. She may even get charged with voluntary manslaughter instead of first-degree murder. Do you remember Jodi Arias, who killed her boyfriend, Travis Alexander? When the story broke, she told the police that two masked individuals had broken into the house and killed Travis. When that lie unraveled, she changed her story and said she killed him in self-defense. Ultimately, she couldn't keep up that lie either. The truth was that Jodi Arias lost her sanity, and she purposely killed Travis in a fit of jealous rage.

Had an interviewer decided to use the minimization technique and fall for her good looks and innocent (not so much) big brown eyes, the interviewer may have led her to lie and say she killed her boyfriend out of self-defense. If she were able to use her feminine wiles and convince you that she was telling the truth, perhaps you would have led her to the best defense attorney out there to protect her from going to prison for first-degree murder. And if Jodi's lawyer and ultimately the judge and jury believed her, she may have been charged with manslaughter and sentenced to five years of prison. Unfortunately for Jodi, there was a lot of evidence that ripped apart her cover stories and exposed her for what she was capable of: cold-blooded murder. That is why I never use the minimization method. I also never create hypothetical situations where I tell the POI what they did. If I don't know what the POI did, I will certainly not tell them what I think they did; I will ask them, "What did you do . . . why did you do it?"

When pressed for time to get a confession, some interviewers feel this is the only technique that will work. And although it has worked successfully for some, I avoid this ruse. When I interview someone, especially if they are involved in a crime, I want them to tell me the cold, hard truth. I will certainly not give them a way out of taking responsibility for their decisions and actions.

If that is not enough to deter you from using both minimization and leading questions, then this may: you can influence a person's recollection of true memories so that they believe something untrue.

Minimizing what a person has done gives them a way out from taking responsibility and accountability. For example, let's say you are the head of HR at a company whose mission is to train individuals from outside organizations in a technical skill. Two female adult students attended a class that your company hosted. They submitted formal complaints about one of the instructors working for your company. This instructor is around sixty-five years of age, and the two students are in their late twenties. They complained that the instructor touched them inappropriately and was too hands-on with them. When you question the instructor, whom you have known for a year, you, as the HR manager, can't imagine these allegations being true because this instructor has a solid reputation and is very professional. You have to interview him because that is company policy. As you are interviewing him, you ask, "What happened? I know you are from a different generation where it was okay to hug females and put your arm around them, but these are different times, and you can't do that. It's inappropriate." Some of you may think that was an effective way to segue into this uncomfortable topic, but guess what? You have just given the instructor an excuse for his actions. What if you didn't know him as well as you thought, and he was touching the young ladies inappropriately? Now you'll never know unless those two students take their formal complaint a step further or another student is brave enough to come forward and submit a formal complaint.

Instead of telling people what they did or why they did it, all you should do is ask them what they did or why they did it. Have confidence in your ability to maintain rapport, sound empathetic, and be respectful. A good interviewer can ask a straightforward question without repercussions from the POI by being nonaccusatory, non-judgmental, and unbiased. Do you think I told the detainees I interrogated, "I know you had to blow up the Twin Towers because of your ideology"? No way!

Instead of telling people what they did or why they did it, use my technique so that you can obtain the truth, no matter how embarrassing, uncomfortable, or incriminating it is. Here is an example of how to use Don't Tell, Ask: Say you are a police officer interviewing a suspected rapist. You would not say, "You were drunk. You probably forced yourself on her." Because what if he did mean to rape that girl? Instead, you would ask, "What did you do to that girl?" or point-blank, "Why did you rape her?" If you have evidence that his DNA was in her, there is no reason why you cannot ask him to-the-point questions. If you don't make a big deal out of it, they won't make a big deal out of it! If you skirt the issue, get tongue-tied, or display any signs of nervousness, verbally or nonverbally, they will perceive you as uncomfortable with the question, so they will be uncomfortable answering it. That means you have to be aware of your body language, eye contact, tone of voice, and the words you use. Any indicator of insecurity on your part will cause the same reaction in the POI. In chapter 3, I talked about how mirror neurons can cause us to mirror the behaviors of others so that we start to experience others' emotions ourselves. As the interviewer, you need to set the stage for the interview atmosphere, which includes an acceptance and appreciation for talking about uncomfortable topics.

If you still feel uncomfortable about bluntly asking, "Why/when did you rape her?" then ask a different question that will get you the same answer: "What exactly did you do to her?" "How did you penetrate her?" Phrasing it this way seems nonaccusatory and almost distances the action of rape from the POI, allowing them to talk more freely about what they did.

Sometimes interviewers will use softening language to help the POI feel more comfortable talking about an event. In this case, softening language would sound like this: "What was going through your mind when you forced yourself on her?" Softening "rape" to "force yourself" may make the POI feel more comfortable talking about the rape because it does not seem as harsh of an event now. However, I am not always a fan of this technique because the POI may cling to your definition of "forcing" rather than openly admitting to "raping." It may be necessary in some cases when you are interviewing juveniles or people with mental disorders, but for the most part, I do not soften language when I ask a question. In my experience questioning litigants (on the TV show I worked on for three years), I found that when I asked them bluntly, "How many times did you cheat—by cheat, I mean to have sexual contact with other men—on your husband?" they appreciated my frankness and honesty. I had nothing to soften or hide from them, and they understood that when I spoke openly, they could speak frankly. It allowed them to feel more secure because they felt I accepted them for who they were. I wasn't judging or blaming them. I had to talk about embarrassing content that had me asking questions about sexual positions and sexually transmitted diseases, but I did it without shying away from those topics. When they saw I was comfortable, they would be at ease going into details even though my inside voice was saying, "I can't believe I am talking about this right now with a straight face." Media hosts often use softening language. They shy away from being direct, and unfortunately, they usually give a person a way to bluff or skirt the details because they want the person to keep talking. Granted, that is their job; they are not out to collect a confession. If they shut a person down, they shut the interview down, and TV networks do not like that.

To further comfort suspects during an interview, I often tell them that I don't care what or why they did what they are being accused of. I make sure to tell them, however, that I need to know precisely what

they did and why. I would let them know I was not there to cast judgment on them; a judge would do that later. I was there to collect all the
information about the event and appreciated their honesty with me.
I also avoided saying things like, "You didn't mean to do it," or "You
had no choice." Those statements appear to give the POI unwarranted
sympathy, especially for something they did that violates human morals and ethics. And in most instances, the suspect had a choice to commit the crime. Even when people lie, it is a choice. The decision to
suppress the truth and tell a lie is a choice. And if you are older than
seven years of age, the age of reason, you know right from wrong, in
most cases. Personality disorders can impact reasoning.

Usually, when interviewers use the minimization technique, they
have to create a story around the information they are after. For example, say your high school student didn't complete their homework
assignment on time, again, and you have to find out why without
sounding accusatory. Minimization would sound like this: "I understand it is difficult to stay focused during COVID and to learn from
home, but you still must complete your homework assignments on
time. Why is it late?" Don't Tell, Ask allows you to ask the question in
a non-accusatory, polite manner: "Why didn't you submit your homework assignment on time?" No story, no feeding them answers.

Let's say you are a senior VP of sales, and one of your clients expressed that they may go with your competitor. Minimization would
sound like this: "Listen, I understand that times have been uncertain
with the pandemic, and that may be causing you some doubt as to
whether or not you can afford to keep up our service. I will tell you,
though, none of our competitors can offer you what we do at our level
of expertise. And, if you suspend your contract and decide to come
back, it will cost you double to reinstate the service because the prices
have increased. When you came on board, you got a great deal, but that
deal no longer exists." That may sound like a normal conversation a
salesperson would have with a worried stakeholder. However, here are
the problems: first, you told them why they do not want to stay on with

you as a client, and second, although what you said may be true, you gave the stakeholder no way to feel like they decided for themselves.

Right now, you enforced their feeling of doubt, and it comes across as though you made their decision for them. That could make the stakeholder feel pressured and backed into a corner. What does a frightened animal do when backed into a corner? Act upon fear and attack. Your stakeholder may act upon fear and terminate their service with you. This way, they may feel that you can no longer threaten them (which is how they may have perceived what you said) or cause them fear. A better way to have this conversation with your stakeholder is to say something like, "I hear you, and I want to thank you for being honest with me about your concerns. Before you make any decisions, let me work for you. Let me answer your concerns because I know I can, and then you can decide to stay with us." You don't pressure or threaten. You let them know that the decision is ultimately up to them, and you know they will make the right one. This way, you make the stakeholder feel empowered, not powerless. And you do not tell them why they are concerned. Let them tell you, and you fix it!

Let me go back to the question at the beginning of this chapter: What more would you need from a suspect who admitted to committing murder? You would want to know how and why they killed this person, who else knew, who else assisted, who else was there, and what will happen now that they committed murder. Is someone coming to avenge the murder? What series of events will happen as a result of the murder? This information will help analyze future crimes.

This chapter is very near and dear to me because one of my biggest pet peeves is hearing interviewers tell a person what they did and why they did it when the interviewer does not know this information. I hope that you try out my technique. I will guarantee (yes, that is how much I trust my technique that I have used since 2002) you will get better results and more honest answers. Remember, we are not just looking for a confession; we are looking for information about the confession and details about the crime, or activity, to which they confessed.

• • •

"Wise men speak when they have something to say; Fools
because they have to say something."

—PLATO

ACTIVITY

Here are three scenarios for you to read and then develop an
alternative Don't Tell, Ask statement/question to replace the
minimizing-the-event statement. The minimization will be
underlined in each example. The answers will be listed in
Appendix C.

SCENARIO #1: COWORKER CLASH

You are the new COO of a start-up company. This is a new
position, and the CEO hasn't informed all stakeholders about
your job. In your position, the HR director reports to you, but
he doesn't know that yet. The first week you are there, you
ask him to meet with you to discuss roles and responsibilities as well as the mission and vision of the company. He is
visibly stressed and tells you he does not have time. Now, he
happens to have an established relationship with the CEO
because he worked for her years ago in another company.
You find out that he went behind your back and complained
to the CEO that you were pressuring him when he had tons
of work to do. The CEO came to you and asked why you
were pressuring him. You explained that you asked to meet
with him to learn more about his role and responsibilities to
work effectively with him. The CEO told you to figure out
how to work with him because she doesn't want him to become upset and quit. So you write him an email that says,

"Good Morning, Rodney, as the new COO, I am excited to work together to take this company to success. I know you are very busy, especially since we are in the beginning stages of establishing this company. However, as your senior supervisor, I need to meet with you for fifteen minutes this week. I would like you to brief me on your position to learn more about your role and initiatives. I know you are stressed and that's why you went to the CEO and complained about me. I am not here to cause you stress; I am here to help alleviate it. Please let me know when we can meet by the end of business today. Thank you, Sincerely, Alicia."

Your task is to rewrite this email following the Don't Tell, Ask rule.

SCENARIO #2: TIGHT-LIPPED WITNESS

You are a detective interviewing a witness to a neighborhood crime. You say, "Listen, I get that you don't want to talk because you fear that the people who did this may come after you. But if you don't tell us what you saw, they will continue to vandalize the neighborhood or, worse, hurt people. Do you want to let that happen?"

Your task is to rewrite this conversation following the Don't Tell, Ask rule.

SCENARIO #3: ADDICTED PATIENT

Disclaimer: I am not a doctor, nor do I speak for doctors. This is just an example of how to use the Don't Tell, Ask technique.

You are a health provider, and you are concerned that one of your patients is becoming addicted to Percocet, which you

(continues)

prescribed him after his surgery. He seems drowsy, incoherent, and there is a change in his personality, but he claims to still be in severe pain, which he shouldn't be after this much time has passed since his surgery. The patient is in your office and is requesting a refill. You approach your concern by saying, "You should not be experiencing pain this long after the surgery. I know that some people are afraid to go off the medication for fear of re-experiencing the pain, but I can assure you, you will feel just fine. I suggest stopping the Percocet for a week, and we'll see how you feel after that."

Your task is to rewrite this conversation following the Don't Tell, Ask rule.

7

ELICIT INFORMATION, DON'T ASK FOR IT

THIS IS A book on interviewing and negotiating techniques, so you are probably wondering why the title of this chapter says, "elicit information, don't ask for it." Sometimes, no matter how much effort you put into planning and preparing for an interview, there will be some people who will not open up to you. They may willingly answer questions about one topic but shy away from another. They may be tight-lipped because they inherently do not trust others. They could be introverted and shy. They may be cooperative and truthful but still not forthcoming with the detailed information you need. Thankfully, there is an elite intelligence tradecraft technique called elicitation that can be the solution.

Elicitation is used by human intelligence services worldwide. According to the Human Intelligence Collector Operations Field Manual, "Elicitation is the gaining of information through direct interaction with a human source where the source is not aware of the specific purpose for the conversation. Elicitation is a sophisticated technique used when conventional questioning techniques cannot be used effectively." It is the planned and inconspicuous acquisition of specific information from a targeted individual, whether face-to-face, over the phone, or via the cyber domain. Elicitation uses provocative statements, not questions, to gain information. If carefully planned and successfully executed, your target will have no worries about sharing information with you. I know this all seems a bit cloak and dagger, but if you trust me to teach you this technique, you will realize elicitation is not sneaky; it is a planned and controlled conversation that conceals intentions.

Questions themselves can put a person on guard because they may come across as intrusive. If you ask too many, the POI may also feel like they are being interrogated. Questions also draw attention to the type of information you are trying to collect. Elicitation allows us to obtain information in a conversational manner that builds rapport, relaxes the POI, and gains their trust without revealing the information we are after.

Think of elicitation as an auspicious way to gather information that is not readily available to the public or too sensitive to ask for directly. Elicitation allows you and the POI to share information in the form of a friendly conversation.

I was trained in elicitation early in my career as a human intelligence officer. I used it when I was an interrogator at Camp Delta in Guantanamo Bay. Although I was trained in approach methods and question techniques to gather intelligence, elicitation allowed me to gather more information because it is a nonaccusatory, rapport-based technique. It worked brilliantly because the detainees assumed I wasn't collecting details, only having a conversation, so their guard dropped.

Based on my intelligence training and the work of John Nolan, who wrote *Confidential: Business Secrets—Getting Theirs, Keeping Yours*, whom I worked for, I have been using, teaching, and perfecting elicitation for decades in both criminal investigations and business intelligence. I even created a new elicitation technique I refer to as the "Help Me" technique. All elicitation techniques are created in the form of provocative statements. The intention of elicitation is to provoke a person to want to respond to your statement. Elicitation allows you to collect data, which can be sensitive, without having to ask for it. This way it doesn't appear that you are collecting information.

My clients come from many industries including sales, marketing, finance, and law enforcement. In the private sector, elicitation is used as a business intelligence tool to help leaders make informed decisions. For example, marketers may want to acquire information on future market forecasts, health professionals may want to find out what is troubling patients, and executives may want to obtain information on their competition. Law enforcement personnel can use elicitation to gather information from witnesses to help solve crimes, collect information from a neighborhood during canvassing operations, or coax a suspect into a confession.

There are many ways you can apply elicitation in your professional and personal lives. Do you want to gain the upper hand in a negotiation? Would you like to know when someone is trying to avoid being truthful or withholding pertinent information that can impact a critical decision you have to make? Do you want to create a relaxed environment so you can draw out information from someone who may be hesitant to share? Elicitation can do all of that.

WHY USE ELICITATION?

There are some situations where you cannot ask for sensitive information such as personal views and industry knowledge. If you do, these questions may seem rude, abrupt, and accusatory. They may put your POI on guard.

Because questioning can pigeonhole a conversation, if you mix in elicitation techniques, you can keep your POI engaged longer, exploring new avenues of significance. If your POI knows you want to interview them, they may say they only have five minutes to give you because they expect it to be uncomfortable. But if you build rapport and have an unassuming conversation that appears to be casual, they are more likely to give you more of their time.

There are times when people are too scared to tell you how they feel or what they know. Patients may feel too embarrassed to discuss health problems with health professionals. Eyewitnesses may be afraid to point out the perpetrator because they fear retaliation. By not asking questions, you create a more comfortable environment for them to disclose sensitive information.

WHY DOES ELICITATION WORK?

Elicitation takes advantage of human psychology and human nature. Most people want to be polite, honest, and trustworthy. Consequently, they tend to open up more around people they perceive to be polite, honest, and trustworthy. People also like to hear themselves talk, educate others, correct others, and show off what they know. If you can entice a person to talk about themselves, you may not be able to stop them from talking.

Another thing most of us like to do is vent our frustrations about things that bother us. If others feel the same way, we tend to feel validated. When we are around others who vent about the same thing, we tend to spill more information because of the common ground and immediate trust we feel toward someone like us. When we become emotional, we can be less discreet with information and can underestimate its value. We may slip and share sensitive data. I'm sure you have heard someone say, "You didn't hear this from me, but . . ." and then go on to share some juicy news.

Finally, most of us want to feel appreciated and valued for who we are, what we know, and how we do things. We tend to seek recognition and respond kindly when we receive it. We will even expand on a topic when given praise because we are on our soapbox and other people are listening. It makes us feel important.

Now that you understand why elicitation works, let's discuss the characteristics of an effective elicitor.

WHO MAKES AN EFFECTIVE ELICITOR?

Anyone can elicit information. But there are personality traits and qualities that will help you be effective.

- Confidence in your ability to carry on a conversation using elicitation, especially with people you do not know well or those who may outrank you.
- Patience, because if you rush a conversation, you will make the POI feel uncomfortable and concerned.
- Good listening skills, since your attention has to be in the present moment on the person you are speaking with.
- Conversational skills and curiosity, which allow you to show interest in the person you are eliciting information from. You do not have to be an extrovert, but you have to be interesting, somewhat charismatic, and knowledgeable about a variety of subjects.
- A good memory because you obviously cannot take notes on your casual conversation, and you will need to recall the details of the information you collect.

ELICITATION IN PRIVATE AND PUBLIC SECTORS

In the public sector, government agencies, military services, and law enforcement use elicitation as a means to gather information about upcoming attacks, illegal activities, network affiliations, money laundering, financing, human trafficking, and drug smuggling. We can gather specific information on emerging threats to overseas embassies that validates or refutes assumptions. We can gather information on atmospherics in the community to determine how safe the area is. And we can recruit people to spy on their country.

In the private sector, corporations use elicitation to find out information about their competitors, technical innovations, market predictions, stakeholder values, and customer needs. Elicitation can help broker relationships, form alliances, acquire talent, find out what drives profitability, and increase an organization's overall business acumen to gain a competitive edge.

Whatever industry you are in, you can use elicitation techniques to control a conversation and acquire what you need.

THE EASY EIGHT ELICITATION TECHNIQUES

Although I teach fifteen techniques, all in the form of provocative statements, I am going to share what I call the "Easy Eight" so you can obtain information without asking questions. Although you can use each technique individually, you will find the more you elicit, the more you will start to combine techniques.

1. *Naivete:* Playing naive encourages a knowledgeable individual to educate you. This technique requires ego suspension as you are projecting yourself as unaware or ignorant. However, in some cases, you will not have to pretend to be ignorant or lack experience because you may be genuinely unaware of the information and inexperienced, which is better. Suppose the POI considers themselves an expert and enjoys talking about themselves and their work. This technique will be instrumental because teaching you will make

them feel good. However, some POIs will respond negatively to this technique. These individuals may prefer to be surrounded by like-minded people or those they feel are intelligent, knowledgeable, or as accomplished as them. Example: "I don't think that is possible," "I find it hard to believe," "I'm not sure that could happen."

2. *Flattery:* Flattery can enhance rapport, create positive emotions in others, and encourage people to open up. People like to feel good about themselves, and this technique encourages them to keep talking. But be careful. A little flattery goes a long way. Do not flatter too much because you may come across as insincere and perhaps condescending. Be careful about how you choose to compliment others. Avoid flattering people on their appearance and materialistic objects because that can give off the "creep factor." You could make someone feel very uncomfortable if you flatter them on their appearance. Some of the safest and most effective things to flatter people on are their morals, ethics, courage, education, certifications, hard work, perseverance, projects, research, family life, and how they raise their children. Remember, flattery can be effective on some POIs and ineffective on others. Example: "I admire your approach," "You have tenacity," "What you did took courage."

3. *Interest:* Showing interest in the POI and what they have to say will encourage them to share relevant information because it will make them feel good about themselves. Your interest can be genuine or counterfeit. If you feign interest, be sure you come across as sincere. Otherwise, you will lose your credibility, and your rapport will suffer. Like flattery, a little interest goes a long way; keep it concise and straightforward to maintain your credibility and trustworthiness. Showing interest can uncover mutual interest. If you can discover common ground with the POI, they will most likely

begin to trust you more. The more the POI talks, the better your chances are of discovering common ground. Real common ground allows you to be authentic. Example: "I would like to hear more about that," "That is interesting," "I'm interested to hear what you think."

4. *Quid pro quo:* The Latin translation is "this for that," meaning, I give you information, and you give me information. The simplest form of quid pro quo that we use every day is when we meet someone: we give them our name, and they give us theirs. Think about the information you want and what you can share that is similar to it. For example, if you're going to find out what your POI's favorite sport or hobby is, it is easy to say, "I like skiing," in hopes that they respond with something in kind, like, "Oh, I like tennis." But sometimes, quid pro quo isn't that easy. You may have to be a little more creative. To encourage a smooth transition and credibility, you should create a story around your provocative quid pro quo statement. For example, if you wanted to find out someone's hobby, create a story around it instead of just coming out and sharing yours. "I am thankful summer is finally here. I have been itching to get back on the water. There are few things in life I can't live without, and sailing is one of them!" This way, your provocative quid pro quo statement does not seem too abrupt and awkward inside a conversation.

    When using quid pro quo, you may find people want to one-up you with an experience or an embarrassing moment. Let them! You are exploiting the instinct some people have to one-up others. Example: "I will tell you about a time when I . . ." "When I was young, I didn't always do the right thing. I remember one time . . ." "We are all human, and even I make mistakes. Wait until you hear this one . . ."

    You can use quid pro quo reflectively, meaning the information you share about a topic you want the POI to talk about will be someone else's information because you lack the knowledge or experience to go in-depth. For example, instead of saying, "I heard that to work at the Pentagon you need a top-secret clearance," you would say, "A friend of mine said that if you want to work at the Pentagon, you need a top-secret clearance." This example could transition over to using naivete, but if you feel that the POI would respond better to a person who is "in the know" than to one who is naive, then use quid pro quo reflectively. Here is another example: You want to find out if the POI has access to information on Country X's political stability, but you do not have any knowledge about Country X's political stability to offer. You could offer up information, which may be fabricated, about your colleague who worked as a journalist in Country X and who got the inside scoop. Saying this would give you a plausibility to only knowing a little information. You would not want to disclose that you do not have any information about the topic. If the POI asks you what else you know, you have a way out of having to fabricate details: "She didn't go into more detail; that's all I know."

5. *Assumed knowledge:* This is when you pretend to be in the know about something so that the POI feels more comfortable disclosing sensitive information. If used effectively, it will convince the POI to think, "What's the harm in sharing something with someone who already knows about it?" This technique helps you establish common ground, encouraging them to trust you more. You will have to prove to the POI that you are in the know by using known terminology or slang, or by sharing technical data. You may have to do some research to prepare yourself to use this technique. You can get the assumed knowledge from sources such as publications, news, social media, and other people. Examples: "My friend is a producer for a news station and she told me how

cutthroat that business is." Or, "No one can engineer a reusable rocket like the SpaceX Falcon 9." (Using the name of the rocket, "Falcon 9," puts you in the know.)

6. *Criticism:* Criticize something that the POI is vested in or interested in, so they feel compelled to defend their position. Sometimes they will get emotional while trying to defend themselves and inadvertently leak sensitive information. When you criticize, do not make it personal; that may offend the POI and make them overly defensive. Criticize a process, an organization, a group, a rule, something the media reported, or other people, but not the POI. Criticism can start casually by poking fun at something, but use it with caution as it can backfire, and you could lose rapport. Example: You are eliciting a squadron commander, and you want to find out why there have been so many F-16 crashes this year. You could say, "It doesn't seem like your pilots are getting the proper training to fly those planes." You are criticizing the training, not the pilots or the squadron commander. However, the commander may still take that personally and respond with, "My pilots are the top of the line! The problem is that these planes do not have enough contractor support during the manufacturing process, so we are experiencing electrical shortages, which are causing them to malfunction." So a better thing to say might be, "I feel bad for your pilots having to fly those poorly made jets. It doesn't seem like they can stay in the sky!" In this provocative criticism statement, you criticize the jets, something the commander should not take personally.

7. *Disbelief:* This technique requires you to do just what it says, express disbelief in something. It is effortless to use as we tend to do this unconsciously in conversations. It is advantageous because it entices the POI to justify the truthfulness of

what they said or know. Your disbelief may be real or fake. If it is fake, make sure you are sincere. Also, think about whether or not what you are expressing disbelief in makes sense. If you express disbelief in something considered common knowledge, you may lose your credibility. Like naivete, this technique encourages the POI to want to enlighten you. It works well on people with big egos. Examples: "I don't believe he did that," "I would need to see that to believe it," "There's no way you could design and produce this that fast, but I'd be impressed if you did!" (combining flattery), "That's good in theory, but in reality, it won't work," "There is no way that technology exists," "You couldn't have shot him from that far away."

8. *False information:* Providing false information should persuade the POI to educate you or correct you. In doing so, they are giving you information. Since you are wittingly providing false information, make up information that is believable enough, so it appears to be genuine. When you state something you know is purposely inaccurate, the POI should feel compelled to correct you. Keep in mind, if they are introverted they may need time to process the information you give them before responding, so be patient. The POI could also hesitate because of the sensitive nature of the information. They may know how to prove you wrong but are not sure they want to share what they know. If you create emotion in the POI, they may lose their discretion and share information. Jonathan Cohen, a professor at the Princeton Neuroscience Institute, conducted a study regarding decision making. Using a functional MRI (fMRI) he proved that many people make decisions based on emotion, not reason. So, if the POI is slightly emotional, they may feel less guarded. Remember that creating feelings and emotions in others can

be both effective and ineffective, so take caution. Examples: "I read somewhere . . . [then insert false information]," "That's not what I heard. I heard [then insert false information]," "We have found out [then insert false information]."

CONTROLLING THE CONVERSATION

Not only should you set the tone, the pace, the length, and most importantly, the topics of discussion, but you will also need to guide the conversation. You can use two techniques to effectively guide a conversation to where you want it to go: bridging and transitioning.

It is always easier to guide an ongoing conversation by bridging conversational topics than it is to introduce an entirely new topic out of the blue. When interviewers switch topics suddenly, it can alarm the POI and cause them to put their guard up. To get around that, interviewers need to be able to take the topic the POI brought up, or that is currently being discussed, and bridge it seamlessly to another topic that is unrelated to the original topic. For example, say you are interviewing a potential job candidate and you have to find out if she has ever violated the law in the past. She mentions that her favorite TV show is *Magnum, P.I.* You need to take the topic of *Magnum, P.I.* and bridge it to the topic of criminal charges so that it looks like a natural progression. Perhaps you can talk about how Thomas Magnum can always get a confession and how his suspects always feel better being honest, which can segue to how honesty is required for this job.

Sometimes we need to transition back to previously addressed topics that were not discussed at length because the POI began to shut down. Perhaps the POI purposely took you off that topic because they did not want to discuss it. If you need to transition back to a topic, say things such as, "You said something earlier that I am still thinking about," or, "What you just said reminded me of something you said earlier."

There will be other times when we need to push the conversation forward because the POI wants to linger on a topic they are comfortable talking about. If you need to transition forward to a new topic, you can say things such as, "That reminds me of something else I haven't asked you yet."

To practice transitioning between topics, try this exercise: Pick two random and unrelated words or topics and bridge them together in six steps. For example, take "snow" to "terror attack in Berlin shopping mall" in six steps: *Snow—Winter—Christmas—Skiing in Europe—Europe unstable—Terror attack in Berlin.* Another example: Take "ice" to "arsonists" in six steps: *Ice—Slang for diamonds—African blood diamonds—Conflict—Kidnapping—Arsonists.* This exercise helps you think on your feet and makes you an effective interviewer.

ACTIVITY

Since elicitation is about making provocative statements, here are eleven statements for you to change into elicitation techniques. The answers are in Appendix C.

1. Where do you come from?

2. Where do you work?

3. What do you think about teenagers' obsession with taking selfies?

4. Do you play sports?

5. What do you like to do for fun?

6. What is your favorite song?

(continues)

7. What is your method to flipping houses and selling at such a high profit?

8. Why do you always have to have the last word in every conversation?

9. Why did you not tell the truth when you had the chance?

10. What is your nickname?

11. There have been four Tesla crashes in the past two months. What is wrong with them?

8

OVERCOME CONVERSATIONAL CHALLENGES

BET YOU HAVE heard that two things are unavoidable in life: death and taxes. Well, there is a third thing: conflict. Whether in the workplace or at home, disagreements happen because, as humans, we think and act differently, have different personalities, and prefer different ways of social interaction. We don't all handle change or communicate the same way. Although our world could not function without diversity, dissimilarities can cause unwanted and unnecessary friction. Sometimes we can avoid it, and sometimes we have to learn to manage it.

When dealing with conflict, first and foremost, always do your best to remain emotionally controlled. This is easier said than done. If we can keep our emotions stabilized, we can maintain a non-accusatory, respectful, and empathetic approach to a conversation. These are the fundamental communication skills we all should strive to embody. Our emotions will try to take over these necessary skills, so we need to exercise our intellect to control our reactions and express our feelings without becoming defensive. Notice I did not say "control our emotions." That's because we cannot. We can, however, control our

reactions to them and regulate how we express them.

When we experience tense emotions such as fear and anger, our limbic system activates our fight-or-flight response. This is good if we are in a life-threatening situation; not so good if we are interviewing, negotiating, or having a talk with our significant other. If we are triggered to fight or flight, our brain's priority is to figure out how we can stay safe. The brain is concerned about our health and helping us stay alive, so it focuses on our breathing, our level of alertness, and maintaining our bodily functions. When all of that is okay, the brain considers our emotions.

If we are overcome with emotions, our limbic system may override our rational, thinking brain. When a perceived threat or stress is severe, the part of the limbic system called the amygdala, a set of neurons best known for its role in processing fear, acts so fast that it can overpower our brain's frontal lobes, which we use to make sound judgments and decisions. So, what happens when we cannot consciously control the amygdala's response to fear? We may say and do things without thinking that we regret later. Let's investigate the limbic system to see how our biology can impact our ability to be rational in times of stress.

When we experience fear, which can happen during a contentious conversation, our bodies quickly activate our stress response system. According to the National Institute for the Clinical Application for Behavioral Medicine, when we feel stress, the amygdala senses our anxiety and sends a distress signal to the hypothalamus. The hypothalamus controls our bodily functions, including releasing stress hormones from our pituitary gland. Once the hypothalamus is activated, our stress response system kicks into gear. The hypothalamus triggers the pituitary gland to secrete hormones that travel from the brain to our adrenal glands located on top of our kidneys. Our adrenal glands secrete adrenaline, norepinephrine, and cortisol into the bloodstream. These stress hormones help prepare our bodies for fight or flight by helping push blood to our muscles, heart, and other organs. Blood carries oxygen, so small airways in our lungs expand, and we can take in more air. The extra oxygen helps keep us alert. So you may be wondering, what's the problem if we are more alert? The issue is our limbic brain can take over our rational/thinking brain. If that happens, our thinking brain's capacity to handle tasks such as listening objectively, speaking clearly, using good judgment, making wise decisions, responding without emotion, avoiding accusations, and saying hurtful things is lost along with other cognitive abilities.

To be able to handle your emotions effectively will require you to be calm. Now that sounds easy, right? We are all wired to respond to certain situations and people automatically—usually due to our biases, assumptions, and expectations. Unfortunately, some of us have become addicted to the chemicals released in our bodies during times of stress. Because of this, we may unwittingly seek or create situations in which we can be angry to experience those chemicals again. Either way, to change habitual unproductive emotional reactions, we have to work on changing our brain's chemistry. Can it be done? Yes. But it will take effort on your part to create new neural pathways.

Now that you understand the body's stress response system, I want to share four actions you can take to change your brain's chemistry. They will allow you to check in with yourself first before you try to diffuse an argument.

1. *Put your brain on pause.* Instead of immediately reacting upon hearing something, pause before you do, say, or think anything. We can only analyze a situation or conversation objectively if we are rational. If we do not add that pause, we could become irrational, make assumptions about others, and even create stories about why someone said something. We have all been there at one time or another because we are human. We want to make sense out of things. Say

your significant other should have been home from work an hour ago. You haven't heard from them. Dinner is ready and getting cold. The kids are hungry. What do you do? You call them, and you barrage them with texts. "Hello?" "Where are you?" "Dinner's on the table." And what if you don't get a response? You become concerned, worried, or angry. Many of us will make up hypothetical situations about why our partner is late. And sometimes, we may play the victim instead of giving them the benefit of the doubt. We may immediately try to fill in the blanks because our brain wants to fill in the information void; it doesn't like not knowing. So, when they finally come home, how do you greet them? Warmly because you were worried about them? Or a little cool because you were perturbed at the lack of courtesy for not responding? If you were a little cool, there is nothing wrong with you. Your limbic brain may have taken over and didn't allow you to think rationally. So, when a dispute arises, take a pause. Remove your emotions as best you can. Hear the other person's side of the story. If you don't know why they said or did something, then find out. Ask straight-forward, concise questions: "Why are you an hour late?" If you find yourself telling someone what they did, why they did it, and worse, what they are feeling, then be prepared for a defensive retaliation. They may have stopped to help people who were in a car accident.

2. *Listen objectively, without your internal voice.* It is difficult to divide our attention between listening and thinking about what we want to say. Usually, one or the other falls off our radar. To listen and retain accurate information, we must quiet our internal voice. Our minds will wander; you will not avoid that, but you can control it. When your mind wanders off from listening to someone, bring your attention back to what that person is saying. A great way to keep your focus is

to repeat what they are saying inside your head. You will eventually be able to stop and just listen. But if you find your attention wandering off for a bit, go back to parroting them with your internal voice until your attention is back on track. There is nothing more frustrating than talking to someone, especially during an interview or negotiation, and knowing they are not listening to you.

3. *Own your part and your actions.* If you say or do something that caused the other person to become angry, defensive, or hurt, you must be willing to take responsibility. If someone tells you they didn't appreciate your tone of voice or the terms you presented, don't blame them for being honest with you. Be thankful! Because now you know you have to change your tone or your terms. Accept their feedback without becoming defensive. They just did you a favor by helping you be a better communicator!

4. *Focus on what you can control (not on what you can't!).* Sometimes, unwittingly, we try to control things that are out of our control. Can you control people? No. So don't waste your time trying. Can you change a person's beliefs? No. There are things in life you can control, and there are things you cannot. Spend your time on the things you can influence. For example, the COVID pandemic, a presidential election, immigration policies, and the Black Lives Matter movement made 2020 a trying year for the United States. In my opinion, it has made many Americans angry and intolerant. I don't dare state my political party affiliation to anyone outside my family for fear of fueling the fire of someone who has a lot of anger regarding politics. Is it my fault they are angry? No, but I know not to poke the bear. I can't change how people react to politics. So what can I change if I want to avoid being ridiculed and barraged with hateful comments for my political stance? I can choose whom I share it with. It is that simple.

Instead of worrying about the other person's emotions, when it comes to negotiation, focus on controlling your emotional reactions. Instead of being concerned about the other person's ego, focus on suspending yours. You will find the more you focus on the things you can influence, the more influence you will have. Make a list of issues that you can and cannot control. Let go of what you cannot control and focus on the things you can. You can control conflict. Instead of focusing on the other person's reactions when in a dispute, concentrate on your own. Instead of worrying about the other person's emotions, control yours. You will find the more you focus on the things you can influence, the more influence you will have.

FOUR COMMON
CONVERSATIONAL CHALLENGES

In each of the following four scenarios, I will provide solutions you can use to help you increase your emotional and conversational intelligence.

1. *POI refuses to engage.* What if the person you are interviewing shuts down and stops talking? Maybe their gaze has moved to the floor or their hands. My go-to technique is to call out the elephant in the room; they know they are not engaging, and you know they are not engaging, so there is no secret. In a nonadversarial manner, call them out on their silence. Address it and move on. Use an elicitation technique from the last chapter, such as naivete: "You know I am not a mind reader. So, if you don't speak, I won't know your side of the story." You may want to use the Help Me technique and say, "Help me understand your point of view. I will listen to

you without judgment." They have shut down for a reason, so be careful not to say anything that will encourage them to strengthen their resolve by remaining quiet. I encountered this numerous times during my interrogations at GTMO. In those days, there were a lot of uncooperative detainees with an "us vs. them" mentality. Often I was told through an interpreter, "I'm not talking; it's in my file." Since I obviously couldn't make them talk, I had to be clever with my techniques. I found that dropping the interrogation approach and adopting a conversational slant worked. I had to change my mindset too. It wasn't me against them; it was me *and* them. This paradigm shift allowed me to be more relaxed and less determined to get them to talk. So if you find yourself in an interview, negotiation, or conversation where the other person has shut down, go back to rapport. If they are still quiet, comment on the fact that they have stopped communicating. If that doesn't work, ask nonpertinent open-ended questions to get them talking about anything, or you could stop asking questions altogether and use elicitation: "I may have just said something that offended you, which was not my intention." And then follow up with an open-ended question such as, "What can I do for you?" Remember, the goal is to get the other person talking about anything at first then about the topic you want to exploit. You may have to listen to them complain or talk about their favorite TV show for a chunk of time, but as long as you can get them to talk, you can get them to answer your questions. Be patient with yourself and them.

2. *You become emotional.* Validate your emotions by accepting why you are experiencing the emotion, then manage it by responding, not reacting. Consider also how the other person feels; both of your feelings are valid. Manage your response to criticism and do not defend yourself. Instead, just provide

information or ask questions. For example: "I want to be sure I fully understand your perspective, but I'd like to also share mine with you." If you feel you are about to lose control of your emotions, try mindfulness techniques such as a calming breath to regain your composure.

3. *Your POI becomes emotional.* You know how critical it is for you as an interviewer to remain emotionally calm, so you always act with intention. However, you will encounter angry people who will act emotionally and often irrationally. The late George Thompson, PhD, who trained millions of professionals in his methodology of "Verbal Judo," said, "When a person is angry, they react and the event controls them; when a person is calm, they respond, and they are in control." If you remain calm, you set the tone for the interview, and you can influence the POI to start to calm down. Never let the POI's anger and emotions get the best of you. Suspend your ego and remain calm. However, some POIs may not relax by mirroring your calm demeanor, so you may have to try another approach. You could say these things to help your POI work through their negative emotions:

"I hear you; I am listening."
"You have a right to your emotions and feelings.
    You have a right to feel that way."
"Tell me exactly how you feel."

Do not try to reason with an angry person. They are not listening intellectually; they are reacting emotionally. You have to calm them down before you can expect them to listen to you.

4. *The conversation takes a destructive turn.* First, recognize any verbal disrespect and escalated emotions without becoming defensive. You may want to acknowledge that you are both human, and you both make mistakes, become emotional, get

angry, and become irrational. Second, try to reframe the conversation to get it back on track. Go back to the topic before it took a destructive turn. "We are not speaking respectfully to each other. Can we go back and talk about XYZ again and then approach this topic being respectful with each other like we have been?" When you anchor a conversation back to a topic where you both had positive or neutral emotions, it won't make sense to bring negative emotions to that particular topic, so the negativity usually dissipates quickly. You can also say, "Let's find a solution together to get back to having a respectful conversation. What do you suggest?" Or rephrase unhelpful statements, like blaming, into helpful ones to create progress. For example, if they say, "Well, you are the one who brought this up, so it is your fault we are arguing," you can say, "I may have taken the wrong tone. I would like us to be able to discuss it still; I'm open to hearing how you think we can approach it."

I want to share a personal story with you about how I came close to losing my cool and destroying a professional relationship. Years ago, I joined a team of instructors I had never worked with before on a new contract for the government. I had to observe a few classes before I was allowed to facilitate them. During one class I was observing, the instructor asked for my feedback, and I shared my opinion on the discussion. After class, he pulled me aside and reprimanded me for what I had said. I was appalled. Apparently, we had a difference of opinion. The old Lena, who was not as emotionally intelligent as the new Lena, would have unleashed fury on him and defended my stance. But I knew better because that behavior was never productive in my past. I chose to listen to him objectively without my emotions. I told myself, "He is not out to hurt you; what he is saying is very important to him, and he took what you said personally. You are not at fault. And he has a right to his emotions. Instead of becoming defensive, help him work through his emotional reaction." I remained calm, suspended my ego, and after he was done speaking, I simply said, "I hear you and value your feedback." He seemed stunned that I didn't defend myself. At that moment his entire demeanor changed. He explained his stance and then offered to provide me with reading material to understand his position better. That day could have taken a destructive turn if I had let it. But I didn't. Ironically, we became great friends, and are still friends today.

If you exercise the techniques in this chapter the next time you are in a disagreement, you will effectively de-escalate it to avoid conflict. These methods will help you work toward creating mutually respectful relationships.

• • •

"The single biggest problem in communication is
the illusion that it has taken place."

—GEORGE BERNARD SHAW

ACTIVITY

Here is a challenge scenario. Come up with three questions you could ask the other person that could be possible solutions to the challenge. These questions should persuade the person to open up. Be mindful of your words and how you come across! You do not want to sound accusatory or judgmental. The answer is in Appendix C.

CHALLENGE SCENARIO

Bob is a project manager who came to you, the program manager, about an incident with one of his team members. Bob told you he overheard his team member, Matt, say, "I'm so sick of COVID! The rules keep changing and no one has any idea what to do. First they force us to get inoculated, so we don't have to wear a mask, now they say we have to even if we got the vaccine. The world is ridiculous!" Bob provided Matt timely feedback, but Matt didn't seem to care what Bob had to say. Now Bob is concerned. He is asking you to speak to Matt. What could you say to Matt to diffuse his emotions and increase his empathy? You will see my response in Appendix C.

9

EMPATHIC NEGOTIATION SKILLS

SOME PEOPLE DREAD having to negotiate, especially when purchasing a new vehicle or selling a home. Others love it. If you ask my parents, they will probably tell you I was born to negotiate. I negotiated to get a cat (when my mom had a *no-pet* rule), a later curfew, and a high school trip to London. Heck, I even negotiated the bedroom I wanted with my two siblings when my parents remodeled the house.

When I was young, I realized how easy it was to get what I wanted if I said the right thing. I couldn't just wing it, though; I had to play out the conversation in my head before it actually took place. I thought of the possible resistance from the other person and how I could deflect it. I also thought about the why. Why would my parents extend my curfew? What's in it for them? And I was never pushy or aggressive because I learned that made the other person defensive or unwilling to negotiate.

Years later, I didn't realize how much negotiation I would be doing as an interrogator in GTMO after 9/11. I never thought of interrogation in that way. I knew I would be using clever approach strategies and questioning techniques, but I was surprised at how much I relied on negotiation tactics. My three-step goal for every interrogation was to build rapport, gain trust, and collect truthful intelligence information. But getting the truth was a negotiation because the detainees weren't going to just give it to me. I had to give them something in return. As I mentioned in chapter 4, that something was directly linked to their personal behavioral drivers, motivations, and needs. I wanted the truth in exchange for what the detainee desired. If I didn't know the detainee's needs, I was at a disadvantage. So I had to ask, not guess. (I had to ask, not tell!) After all, when you are trying to find out when the next attack on American forces overseas will be, you do not have time to waste. If I assumed I knew what was driving the detainee's behavior not to tell the truth, I could have become frustrated and ruined any chances of rapport and trust. For example, if I had assumed a detainee wanted to be set free of the guilt he felt from lying, but what he really wanted was to die as a martyr inside Camp Delta, I would have gotten nowhere.

Here is a four-step process that helps me frame my thoughts and avoid making assumptions when I plan interviews and negotiations:

1. *Profile my target:* I discover my target's personality preferences, personal drivers, motivators, needs, and likes/dislikes.
2. *Plan my approach:* What is the first thing I will say? What will my demeanor be? How will I build rapport? How will I persuade them to be open and honest with me?
3. *Plan my conversation:* What do I want? What do they want? What is their *why* for giving me what I want? What if *this* happens? What if they say *that*? How will I respond?

4. *Execute the conversation:* I think about being the three Cs: calm, confident, and charismatic. You do not have to be an extrovert to be charismatic. Charisma is charm; we all can have appeal, and it attracts the attention of others.

This planning helps me to gain the other person's trust. You cannot successfully negotiate if you cannot rely on the other person to be open and honest. Of course, the same goes for you; you have to be open and honest no matter how uncomfortable it may be. So how can you increase your trustworthiness? Do not be afraid to admit to a mistake or take responsibility for something you said or did that had unintended negative consequences. Stand your ground but be fair. Do not enter a negotiation with unjust demands. And do not beat around the bush when it comes to what you want and what you believe you deserve. Always think teamwork. You are not in a battle; you are in a negotiation. You both are in it to win it, so work together to gain a win/win situation. Listen objectively. Remember, if you want to be heard, you have to listen to the other person.

TRUST EXERCISES

- On a scale of 1 to 10 where 1 equals no trust and 10 equals the highest level of trust, rate the following professions: doctor, lawyer, police officer, firefighter, salesperson, teacher. Now write the reason why you ranked them the way you did.
- Think of the people in your life whom you trust and ask yourself why you trust them. Write down five reasons you believe they are trustworthy. Do you embody this quality? Then write down five reasons why others trust you.

KNOWING YOUR OPPONENT'S STANCE

During a negotiation, you must know your opponent's stance. What do they want and what is driving their behavior? When a salesperson is trying to sell you something, say a couch, they aren't selling a piece of furniture; they are selling something to appeal to your emotional driver. Perhaps it is family time watching the Super Bowl together, or maybe it's the place where a person can relax with a good book. Salespeople should sell to a person's driver because people tend to make decisions based on emotion, not reason. Envisioning myself on that couch watching my favorite movie creates positive emotions and releases the feel-good hormone dopamine. I want that feeling, so I buy the sofa.

I recently bought a new car. (How timely as I write this chapter!) First, I had to negotiate with my husband because he was not a fan of the Land Rover Defender that I wanted. Once we took it for a test drive, he was sold. The fact that it was rated the 2021 SUV of the year by MotorTrend probably didn't hurt my stance. I wanted a four-door, but the sticker price was a shocker. My husband said, "If you want this box [he thinks it looks like a box], get the two-door; we already have a four-door RAM." Even though I was paying for the vehicle, I still had to negotiate some terms with him, and I opted for the two-door.

When we initially met with the salesperson before the test drive, I told him I wanted a car that could plow through a snowdrift, drive through a flooded street, and haul all of my animals in case of an emergency. I gave him my personal drivers and he tailored his pitch to all three of them. Instead of talking about the innovative technology, he started with the drive settings (snow/gravel/gradient).

You have to know what people value most and sell to that. It's the same in negotiations. If you know what the other person values, you can use that as leverage. For example, I was in Cabo San Lucas recently, buying trinkets in a store. There was no business to be had in this market square; it was dead. I knew I could use that as leverage when negotiating how much I was willing to pay for what I was buying.

Negotiation is about reaching an agreement benefiting both parties involved. Negotiation can help you get the price you want, get in or out of marriage, get a job, get the truth, and end an argument. Governments, union workers, lawyers, law enforcement, and anyone in a relationship negotiates.

NEGOTIATIONS MUST BE PRINCIPLED

The best negotiators look at the problem objectively without a personal bias and explore solutions. They suppress self-interest and are considerate of the other party. They are fair, professional, respectful, and follow a moral compass. Here are a few ways to maintain principled negotiation standards:

- *Be calm.* Mindfulness tells us that when we are calm, we are more present and aware. Mindfulness practices, such as diaphragm breathing, meditation, practicing gratitude, and being kind, help us guide our attention and increase our awareness about our feelings, emotions, senses, thoughts, reactions, decisions, verbal and nonverbal language, even our intuition. Mindfulness practices also help increase our awareness of others, which is especially helpful during interpersonal interactions. You may want to start with a calming breath: inhale deeply, hold the breath for a few seconds, and then exhale through your mouth. Physiologically, mindfulness can shrink the amygdala and enlarge the hippocampus, an area of the brain that controls memory and learning. Mindfulness can reduce cortisol, lower blood pressure, improve immune system responses, and strengthen the neural circuits responsible for concentration and empathy. You will begin to notice your awareness increasing and your mind clutter decreasing, which in turn will increase your mental agility during a negotiation.

- *Negotiate in person.* When you are face-to-face with someone, you naturally are more empathetic and respectful. When we are on camera, on the phone, or writing emails, we may feel that we can hide behind a shield that protects us from the other person's verbal or nonverbal backlash to an unprofessional or rude comment we made. Feeling protected can give us the false sense that we do not have to mind our manners. To put a governor on your emotions, try if at all possible to negotiate in person to ensure you are on your best behavior.

- *Put yourself in the other person's shoes.* You should be thinking about how the other party will feel about what you want. What could be their resistance and why? How will you address this resistance? Both parties should be able to voice their perceptions and concerns openly and without judgment.

- *Come prepared.* Have statistics, facts, and figures at hand. Know what your opponent wants and their emotional drivers and needs. To go one step further, know their personality preferences and the preferred communication and decision-making styles. Be your own devil's advocate and challenge your negotiation plan and your assumptions.

- *Be prepared to say no.* Do not let the other person persuade you to agree to something you are not comfortable with. You can't get to a yes if you cannot successfully navigate the noes. That means when you are planning this conversation out in your mind, you have to play the devil's advocate. Why might your opponent say "no" to your request? Come up with as many reasons as you can. Then come up with responses to their "no." Say I tell a suspect that I need her to come clean with all the details about the homicide. In exchange for her cooperation, I will personally tell the judge how cooperative she was because she wanted to do the right thing, and because of that, the judge may be lenient. I will challenge my plan by taking an opposing stand. What if the suspect says, "I don't believe you, and I'm not going to say anything else to you. I want a lawyer. They will help me. You won't." Now what? I have to prepare a response. Perhaps this would work: "I hear you. Most people in your position think that way. But do you realize the lawyer works for money, not necessarily for you? I don't make money off of you, so that should tell you that my best interest is in what happens to you, not the fee I can collect." (I mean no disrespect to lawyers!)

- *Use empathetic statements.* Inside your negotiation conversation, throw in empathetic statements such as, "I wish I could do better," or, "I had hoped I could offer you more." This way, you can still hold your ground and come across as sincerely interested in their well-being.

- *Don't be afraid to show vulnerability.* When you expose your weaknesses, faults, and mistakes, people tend to empathize with you. When you expose yourself as "being human," others tend to open up about their own shortcomings. To show vulnerability in a negotiation, you can tell your opponent that in thinking about this negotiation you realized you should have offered less or asked for more because you forgot to factor in XYZ. Let them know you made a mistake and that they are getting a good deal from you, even when you know you got the better deal. By doing this, you can make your opponent feel satisfied with the terms of the negotiation.

- *Use a confident voice.* A confident voice does not mean you are shouting or barking out demands. It means you are lowering your tone and pitch to sound more authoritative, but you still want to come across as warm and friendly. Higher-pitched voices are associated with increased emotions and deception. When lying, some people's voices (like mine) increase in pitch. Science explains why this happens. If you are someone who gets nervous and worried when you lie, then stress hormones are released. As a result, your body experiences physiological responses such as sweating and an increase in pulse. When we experience stress, the muscles in our body tighten, and that includes our vocal cords. So, if your pitch is elevated, you may sound insincere and untrustworthy.

- *Check in with your biases.* "Bias" has become an ugly word, but did you know that every human being has them and that they are evolutionary? They were meant to help us stay alive and safe. However, they can do harm as well. Your biases can cause you to be subjective and judgmental. According to the Oxford Dictionary, a bias is "an inclination or prejudice for or against one person or group, especially in a way considered to be unfair." Our preferences, likes, and dislikes can formulate biases at an early age based on what we pick up from our family, friends, peers, the media, and our experiences. Without realizing it, we can adopt a bias toward a specific type of person or group of people, or even a geographic area.

We know that we are not supposed to judge a book by its cover. But we all do it. Why? Because, again, it is evolutionary. The moment we meet someone, we start making assumptions about them because our minds instantly compare that image (or that voice, if we meet over the phone) to other like images. Maybe these images are from people we have met in the past or have seen on TV. Our brains categorize what we see to figure out if this person is, for example, good, bad, harmful, safe, annoying, funny, or trustworthy. In a way, our brains are trying to protect us because we do not want to get to know a person who could harm us. But we all know that first impressions can be wrong. As long as we do not let that judgment be our deciding factor, we will be able to look beyond our initial decision. The best way to overcome bias is to realize you have one and remain open-minded.

Here are five common biases that could have negative impacts on rapport and communication:

1. *Stereotype Bias* is when we expect a group or a person to have certain qualities without knowing that person. Stereotypes we typically encounter concern gender, language, dialect, dress, hygiene, jobs, hobbies, health habits, body art, hairstyles, where you live, the car you drive, age, and education.

2. *Similar to Me Bias* is when we perceive someone as "like" us because they share something in common with us. Because of that, we automatically like or favor them without knowing who they are. This bias can be concerning when it comes to safety. We may think we have a good rapport with someone and let our guard down when we are with them. Remember, some people purposely try to be like us to gain our trust so they can deceive us. But even people who are similar to us may be dangerous to us.

3. *The Halo/Horns Effect Bias* is when we rate individuals either too high or too low based on a trait, an erroneous overall impression, their role, status, age, job, or popularity. An excellent example is Lance Armstrong. We all believed he couldn't have taken performance-enhancing drugs to win the Tour de France because he was a cancer survivor. Why would someone who beat cancer lie to us? Simple. To win the Tour de France. Examples of the Halo Effect would be if you hear someone say, "She is one of the top-rated scientists on this project, so just deal with her high-handedness." Or, "He is in school to be a doctor; there is no way he would mistreat his girlfriend like that." This is really dangerous in the online dating world. There was a killer who posed as a cop online. Women automatically trusted him because he was a cop. Guess what? He killed five women and almost got away with it. An example of the Horns Effect would be, "She's from New

England; she must be obnoxious and a little rough around the edges. People up there aren't nice."

4. *Confirmation Bias* is when we listen only to information that confirms our preconceptions. Consequently, we disregard any information that may contradict our preexisting views. This bias can have negative consequences when detecting deception. Sometimes interviewers cannot let go of a confirmation that a person is guilty or is lying even though deceptive analysis supports that they are truthful.

5. *Bond Bias* is when you feel part of a group, bonded by likes or dislikes, personality traits, experiences, or commonalities, and you tend to fear and dislike others outside your group even though you don't know them. I see this happen in organizations with a wide range of processes and team divisions. For example, engineers tend to bond together because they all speak the same technical language and work on similar tasks. When someone approaches them from the marketing or sales department, they may not communicate effectively or respectfully with them because of the bond bias. The engineers may view others as "outsiders" and become frustrated with them because they cannot understand their common language. The bond bias can happen when you are with a group of strangers in a stressful environment, and you automatically bond together because you are all experiencing something traumatic. Years ago, this happened to me when I had to take my sick chinchilla to the emergency vet on a Saturday morning. Everyone in the waiting room had a pet with an emergency. We all started talking and bonded together as though we were lifelong friends. If you can create this sense of urgency for someone to connect with you, you will gain their trust. In an interview, you could do this by making the interviewee believe that the room you are in is safe from what is happening outside.

BATNA, WATNA, AND BOND

It is silly to think all negotiations will be successful; they won't. But why set yourself up for failure? You want to position yourself for success. BATNA stands for the Best Alternative to a Negotiated Agreement. It means the best alternative course of action for both parties if an agreement can't be reached. Perhaps each party gets a little something, but it wasn't their desired end result. Some experts say that the alternatives could be better than the original negotiated agreement, which may be accurate. But they could also be worse. That brings us to the WATNA, or the Worst Alternative to a Negotiated Agreement, for when you have to compromise, you don't get what you want, and there is no hope that you will.

BATNA and WATNA have been around for decades. They exist to get two parties to agree on terms when the negotiation isn't successful. One party may indeed get stuck during negotiations because of limitations. They might not have the ability, resources, or means to continue to negotiate. Alternatives can help a party reach a more favorable agreement. Here is an example from my world as an interrogator. I told you I negotiated for the truth, and I had limitations. There were things I couldn't do or offer. If a detainee wanted to get out of GTMO and be sent home, I couldn't promise that. But if they wanted their cell changed or to write a letter to someone, I could do that. So, in essence, the detainee's BATNA may have been for me to move his cell and allow him to write letters home instead of being able to get out of prison. When a negotiation cannot continue, a BATNA is a way through it.

Think of BATNA or WATNA as a backup plan for when negotiations cease. I have no problems considering a BATNA for my opponent, but I don't think in terms of a BATNA on my end. Assuming I will not get what I want and may have to comprise may set me up for failure. Instead, I plan in terms of the Best Outcome in a Negotiated Deal (BOND). Dump the BATNA and WATNA and go with BOND.

When thinking in terms of your BOND, you will shift your mindset going into a negotiation. BOND is what will be best for both parties. First, you are instinctively thinking win/win. And second, you have to figure out why the negotiation is failing instead of going to alternative settlements. Are both parties being up front, realistic, and fair? Are emotions affecting better judgment? Once you figure out the why, you can regroup and go to your BOND.

When thinking BOND, don't give up on your stance. Hold your ground; you obviously have something the other party wants. Always be empathetic to the other party and think win/win. Be magnanimous. Never be aggressive or arrogant. Realize that sometimes it's okay to walk away. Unless it's a hostage negotiation scenario. In that case there is no BATNA or WATNA, just BOND. You can't sacrifice the safety of the hostages. The Best Outcome—the *only* outcome—is to have the hostage-taker surrender peacefully and have all hostages released unharmed. So that is how you plan your negotiation process.

KNOW YOUR NEGOTIATION PARTNER TYPE (NPT)

Based on my expertise in personality types and human behavior profiling, and my decades of real-world experience in interrogation/interviewing and negotiating, I have developed eight negotiation partner types, or NPTs. The three dichotomies I used to create these types are Hard vs. Soft, Experienced vs. Inexperienced, and Extroverted vs. Introverted. All possible combinations create eight types of negotiation partners. Understanding your NPT will help you handle them by knowing how to interact with them verbally and nonverbally. But first, let's define the dichotomies.

A *hard negotiator* is skillful and persuasive, and they can be forceful and pushy. They are out for a personal win and view negotiation as an oportunity for victory. They will try to get as much as they can while

giving little. They have an easy time separating people from the problem. They do not trust others and come to a negotiation ready to fight
and protect themselves.

A *soft negotiator* is passive, friendly, and wishes to avoid conflict. As
a result, they are more yielding and less confrontational. They see negotiation as a bargain where both parties will benefit. They easily
trust others and focus on human relationships; thus, they consider
people part of the issue.

Whether your opponent is hard or soft, experienced or inexperienced, we have four types of negotiators: hard experienced, hard inexperienced, soft experienced, and soft inexperienced. An experienced
negotiator uses principled negotiation tactics; an inexperienced
negotiator will either succumb to you and claim defeat or use unprin-
cipled tactics. They may not be prepared, they may bring along their
biases, they may not be considerate, and they may be out for their own
best interest. If they feel backed into a corner, they may become emotional and not play fair. If they become too emotional, they may lose
their internal moral compass.

Finally, you will have to handle either the extroverted or introverted type in each of these four types. So, in essence, you have a total
of eight types of negotiation partners that you will come in contact
with. There are challenges and benefits to each. I will discuss the characteristics of each one and how to effectively negotiate with them.

HARD EXPERIENCED (EXTROVERTED) (HE-E)

This negotiator will make you work because they have negotiation
skills, and they will be quick to cut you off and dominate the conversation. They are social and good at persuasion tactics. Their charm
can have you eating out of their hand, so you must keep your wits
about you. You may want to slow the rate of your speech, so it slows
them down a bit. Do not be afraid to take control of the conversation.
If they perceive you as weak, they will walk all over you. Hold your

head high and stand your ground. Keep a straight, erect posture with a wide stance. Take up space! Talk with your arms and move about the room. Always keep good eye contact and angle your belly button and your feet directly toward them. It is a signal that you are not afraid to face them head-on. Extroverts appreciate that. Avoid crossing your arms and legs. The moment you do this, the extrovert will feel you are closing off from them. Maintain an open body posture. You can even stand in the Superman or Wonder Woman pose. If you are sitting at a table, sit upright and lean into them. That will show that you are ready for business. Do not hesitate to engage in some small talk as well. Extroverts like to talk. Once you make them feel more comfortable, they will inherently want to bond with you because extroverts get stimulated by outside experiences. If you can connect with the HE-e negotiator, you have a chance at getting what you want because they will use principled negotiation tactics.

HARD EXPERIENCED (INTROVERTED) (HE-I)

This negotiator is like a wolf in sheep's clothing. They are smooth and polished because they naturally think and reflect first, then act. You will have to stay focused when negotiating because the HE-i will be methodological in their approach. They have probably studied and rehearsed all aspects of the negotiation and will try out every possible tactic on you. You do not want to space invade the HE-i or stare them down. They will prefer if you have more closed and quiet body language. They can have sensory overload and appear to shut down if you are too extroverted, or you are with a group of people, or there is too much noise and chaos in the room. This could lead them to pull away from the negotiation table, and you may be stuck searching for your BATNA. If you are planning with a BOND in mind, you will want to ensure you use verbal and nonverbal language to make this person feel comfortable around you. You may wish to speak with a softer voice. Add pauses so they have time to reflect internally on what you are saying. If you don't allow them that time, your message may be lost.

HARD INEXPERIENCED (EXTROVERTED) (HI-E)

This negotiator may drive you crazy and exhaust you. The HI-e relies on other people and other things to hold their ground, but they don't really have the experience to negotiate. They won't care, however. They can talk their way out of anything and make it appear as though they know what they are doing. Do not call their bluff because you may make them defensive, and you could easily upset them. Emotions can run high in the HI-e. If they get overwhelmed with negative emotions, they could become irrational and intense. Deep down, they know they do not possess the skills to negotiate, but they will do everything possible so you never figure that out. This person will take things personally and become aggressive, and you may see them finger-pointing as a convincing technique. They may try to hide their lack of confidence with arrogance. Ignore their behavior and do not take what they say or do personally. Since you want a mutually respectful relationship, do not flash contempt when speaking to them. Contempt shows up on your face as a half-smile or smirk that reveals moral superiority. If they catch on that you feel better than them or are placating them, they may shut negotiations down to get the upper hand. They could resort to hostility if they feel exposed. You should never hide your hands when negotiating because it signals you are not being open and honest. In the body language world, we have a saying: "Hide your hands, hide something!" You will have to be calm and confident as you discreetly teach them how to negotiate fairly. Clarify what they said by repeating it back to them. This will help foster effective communication.

HARD INEXPERIENCED (INTROVERTED) (HI-I)

The HI-i doesn't trust anyone, and they can be very stubborn. They can come across as pushy and inconsiderate. Because they lack trust in their communication and negotiation skills, you have to handle them with care, or else you will feel like you are trying to push a boulder uphill. Be careful not to say or do anything to make them think they are trapped in a corner. This person most likely fears you and the negotiation process, but they are still up for the fight. They may become quiet because they will be internalizing their fear. So your concern should be to gain their trust and keep them engaged. Once they shut down, it will be challenging to get them to open up again. Adopt the same verbal and nonverbal language as you would for the HI-e, but for the HI-i, you want to be patient and calm. Because they are better at concealing their emotions, they can be hard to read. You will have to use the techniques in chapter 11 on body language to help you uncover hidden messages. If they have something to say, allow them the time to say it without interruptions. They will appreciate that, and they won't feel you have dismissed them as incompetent. Help them through the negotiation process by reminding them of the win/win stance. Show them respect to get them to respect you. You may want to use elicitation techniques to help persuade them to be fair and principled. This way they will not take offense when you ask them to be open-minded.

SOFT EXPERIENCED (EXTROVERTED) (SE-E)

This may be an enjoyable experience for you. Because the SE-e is extroverted, they are people-focused. They will have an interest in you and getting to know you. Because they are Soft Experienced, they won't be brash or domineering in a conversation. In fact, they will be friendly and nonconfrontational. They easily trust you because they sincerely want you to trust them. They will have no problem carrying on a witty conversation and using skillful techniques, but they are always thinking about how the process and the outcome of the agreement will affect you. The SE-e has your interest in mind as well as theirs. In my opinion, this is the best opponent to negotiate with because it will be challenging skill-wise but with a friendly, upbeat twist. Be as genuine and as open as you can when conversing. Maintain open body language and use inclusive vocabulary words such as "we" and "us." You can also tell them you appreciate their tactics and enjoy working with them. You may even develop a long-term relationship with this type.

SOFT EXPERIENCED (INTROVERTED) (SE-I)

An SE-i will know the game, but it may come across as though they don't because they will be a bit reserved. They prefer deliberate speaking, so they carefully plan what they will say and how they will respond to you. Because they are Soft, they naturally respect your point of view and perspectives. Don't be fooled by their quiet demeanor. Realize it is their personality preference. They are Experienced. You want to quiet your language, both nonverbal and verbal, when communicating with an SE-i so they warm up to you. Your primary focus when negotiating with an SE-i is to refrain from making up a story as to why you don't trust them. Because they possess negotiation skills, you may tend to think they are up to something underhanded because they are introverted and soft. If you can read their verbal and nonverbal cues, you will be able to identify if they are truthful or not. If you are introverted, you will find it easy to win their trust. You do not want to rush an SE-i in a conversation, so use pauses, relax, and have patience.

SOFT INEXPERIENCED (EXTROVERTED) (SI-E)

This type of negotiator shouldn't be negotiating. Being that they are Soft, they are not going to be pushy, demanding, or self-centered. They would rather build and maintain healthy relationships. Because they are Inexperienced, they may lack the formal training or interpersonal skills needed for this type of communication. Yet they will still be more than happy to engage with you. Being extroverted, they are probably comfortable holding conversations with strangers and being around new people. They may talk excessively to cover up their low skill level. And they may leak sensitive information they shouldn't, which for you will be a benefit. Try not to take advantage of them. If you take advantage of them and they discover you are unjust, you may have consequences to face. The SI-e hopes that their friendliness will persuade you to be fair with them. Follow your moral compass when negotiating with this type.

SOFT INEXPERIENCED (INTROVERTED) (SI-I)

If you are negotiating with an SI-i, you could win almost anything, but you could lose other things, like your reputation. Your primary concern when negotiating with an SI-i is to avoid being overbearing. Make them feel they are competent. You can even make them feel good about their decisions by telling them they made a wise choice. Because they are Inexperienced and Soft, you clearly have the advantage, but don't take advantage of them. Remember, negotiations are principled. We need to be considerate of the other person. One day you may need something from them, and if they think you played them, you might not get it.

Now, you may wonder why you would even care about making an SI-i feel capable, not making an HE-i feel trapped, or not calling the HI-e's bluff. The answer is because you may have to negotiate with them again! Think ahead and prepare yourself to end every interview or negotiation on pleasant terms because you may need something from them in the future.

Remember, negotiation is not a compromise. In a compromise, no one gets what they want. To get what you want, consider your opponent and the best approaches to take with them to establish a relationship in which both parties feel they have won.

• • •

"Let us never negotiate out of fear.
But let us never fear to negotiate."

—JOHN F. KENNEDY

ACTIVITY

For fun, go to a furniture store, a car dealership, or anywhere that you can typically negotiate a price for something. Use this checklist and try to get at least 10 percent off of the sticker price!

PROFILE YOUR TARGET
- What is your NPT? HE-e, HE-i, HI-e, HI-i, SE-e, SE-i, SI-e, SI-i.

PLAN YOUR APPROACH TO AN EMPATHIC NEGOTIATION
- Do it in person, face-to-face.
- Put yourself in the other person's shoes.
- Build rapport.
- Come prepared with facts and data.
- Be prepared to say "no."
- Use empathetic statements to create a safe environment.

(continues)

- Use elicitation techniques to encourage your opponent to open up.
- Don't be afraid to show vulnerability.
- Use a confident voice.
- Check in with your biases.

PLAN YOUR CONVERSATION
- What is your objective?
- What is your BOND?
- What is their *why*?

EXECUTE THE CONVERSATION

10

HANDLING THE BREAKING POINT

N THIS CHAPTER, I want to talk about the point at which the POI is contemplating whether to break and tell the truth or to keep lying and defend their lie. You will know when a person has reached their breaking point because you will see it in their body language and hear it in their voice. There are certain verbal and nonverbal behaviors you will see when a person contemplates whether or not to tell the truth. I will share those indicators with you and statements you can say at that crucial moment to help persuade the POI to open up and give you honest answers.

When a person is at the breaking point, the interviewer can push them over the edge by telling them something like, "Both you and I know the evidence can prove you were there." Or the interviewer can ease up, allowing the POI time to break on their own will by saying something like, "I can see you are concerned about something. You know you have a decision to make, and I know you will make the right one." You may want to ask a question such as, "How are you feeling right now?" Or maybe it's best to say nothing at all. Whichever approach the interviewer takes, they need to create an environment in which the POI feels comfortable. This chapter will prepare interviewers to help the POI make the right choice and tell the truth.

So what does the breaking point look and sound like? How can you know for sure someone has reached it? Let's look at the signs.

NONVERBAL BREAKING POINT ATTRIBUTES

A typical nonverbal indicator of the breaking point is when a person starts to ball up physically. They will slump their shoulders forward, drop their head, and sometimes bend forward, leaning into the interviewer. It can look as though a weight has been put on their shoulders. Lying can cause negative emotions such as guilt, worry, and shame. Consequently, those emotions can create the sensation of a heavy weight, felt emotionally and seen physically. Some POIs at the breaking point may appear to "zone out" from experiencing cognitive overload. Some may not be able to look you in the eye, either from fear of facing you while lying or from fear of you exposing their lie. Most become still.

VERBAL BREAKING POINT ATTRIBUTES

Verbal indicators that a person is at their breaking point could include a refusal to talk because their focus and concentration are on what decision to make. As the interviewer, you may hear signs of stress and nervousness, such as their voice cracking or shaking, their breathing becoming labored from the stress, and the tone and pitch of their voice or even their rate of speech changing. The POI may sigh and take deep breaths.

PERSONAL DRIVERS AND
MOTIVATIONS TO BREAK

To effectively handle the breaking point so that the POI breaks instead of shutting down, you need to figure out what will motivate the POI to confess. Here are examples of some personal drivers and motivators. Your POI may:

- Fear going to jail.
- Fear being killed or harmed by others if they tell the truth.
- Fear the loss of their job or lifestyle.
- Feel embarrassed, guilty, or shameful.
- Not trust the interviewer.
- Believe that if they break, they will be handing their adversary/interviewer a victory.

Some POIs may want to break because of a psychological need regardless of the consequences, such as:

- *Gratitude.* They want to reward you for being kind, non-accusatory, patient, and honest.
- *Relief.* Inherently, people want to be honest; the POI may feel the need to be honest and alleviate the burden of guilt.
- *Reward.* The POI may believe that telling the truth will be the best for their family/friends.
- *Self-respect.* The POI needs to feel good about themselves and finally do the right thing.

During this critical time, you may want to use pauses and soften the tone and volume of your voice. With security and safety in mind first, you may want to use touch to create a sense of togetherness by lightly touching a safe zone area like the arm or leg (only use when the interviewer and POI are the same sex and always abide by cultural norms). Touch can make people feel more connected. You may want to sit closer to the POI. Read their body language to see if the invasion of their space is welcomed or not. Ask the POI questions like, "What can I do to help you?" or, "Is there anything you want to ask me?" Use the pronoun "we" to create a team environment.

The breaking point can come when the POI knows you have discovered their lie. We want to let them know we know they lied, but we don't want to sound accusatory. To do this, you can say: "It appears to me..."

- "... that there is something else you want to tell me." (Avoid saying, "There is something else you are not telling me," because that may be accusatory and cause them to shut down.)
- "... that there is more to the story."
- "... that there is something else on your mind you want to share."

You can also say, "I may be wrong, but..."

- "... I sense some hesitation in your answers."
- "... you appear to be uncomfortable." (You can ask a follow-on question after they answer, such as, "What can I do to gain your trust?" or, "What can I do to make you feel comfortable?")

EMBEDDED COMMANDS

You can also persuade a POI to break by using embedded commands such as, "I notice that when I questioned you about [insert topic]..."

- "... you became nervous."
- "... you looked like you felt guilty."
- "... you looked like you wanted to tell me something."

You can say, "Now that you know I have discovered discrepancies in your story . . ."

- ". . . you are feeling guilty."
- ". . . you want to come clean."
- ". . . you want to tell the truth to relieve the burden you are feeling."

You can say, "Eventually . . ."

- ". . . you will tell me the truth because it is the right thing to do."
- ". . . the burden of lying will be too much for you to handle."
- ". . . you will accept I caught you in a lie; we have evidence that points to you."

You can also say:

- "It's not easy to lie; you will get confused."
- "No one can remember a rehearsed story; you will forget the details."
- "You may notice how worried you feel right now."
- "You are probably starting to think that telling me that lie was a bad idea."
- "You are probably starting to think it's time to come clean and tell me the truth."
- "Remember, everyone leaks indicators of deception, and I am trained to pick up on them."
- "Tell me why I don't believe you."

The breaking point is a pivotal time in an interrogation. Be patient with yourself and the POI. Do not rush your words or become pushy. Relax and trust in your skills to bring the POI to the right decision, to tell the truth. Your choice of words and how you deliver them will make or break your success in persuading the POI to tell the truth.

• • •

"In any moment of decision, the best thing you can do is the right thing. The worst thing you can do is nothing."

—THEODORE ROOSEVELT

11

HOW TO ACCURATELY ANALYZE BODY LANGUAGE

"READ BETWEEN THE lines" is an idiom that suggests a hidden meaning. "Cryptography" comes from the Greek words *kryptós*, which means "hidden" or "secret," and *graphein*, which means "writing." It is the practice of writing, reading, and analyzing secret messages meant to secure communication between two parties and prevent a third party from deciphering the message. An early form of cryptography involved writing with "invisible ink" (usually an acid or chemical) between the lines of unclassified, open text. When the communication reached its recipient, the recipient would use chemicals to expose the secret message.

Analogous to invisible ink, people will conceal true feelings and thoughts within their communication—verbally and nonverbally, wittingly and unwittingly. When we trust others, we take for granted that when they communicate, they are honest and truthful. Human nature wants us to be honest and trust others. However, you know as well as I do, not everyone is trustworthy. Perhaps you trusted an employee to run one of your satellite offices for years, never knowing they were stealing money from you the entire time. You may be interviewing a job candidate who has an undisclosed felony record, a passenger at a checkpoint who is smuggling drugs, or someone else who is concealing the truth.

Many of you have heard of Emotional Intelligence (EI). I will teach you what I call Body Language Intelligence (BLI). When it comes to analyzing nonverbal behaviors, you must first be aware of your own, and then you can learn to assess others accurately. BLI will help you understand how our movements and gestures can shift our attitudes and behaviors. It will also help you discover when people are not honest with you and, most important, how to decipher if someone is stressed or nervous from lying.

In this chapter, you will learn how lies are created and the difference between the two types of liars. I will teach you how to baseline people's behaviors and I'll explain the most accurate indicator of deception.

BECOME MORE AWARE OF YOUR BODY

In an interview or a negotiation, our nonverbals can create a communication barrier that makes others distrust us and turn away. We can inadvertently send a signal that we are not interested in the other person, that we feel superior to them, that we are not open to hearing their thoughts, that we are defensive or aggressive, or that we are not honest, even when we are. Although we are supposed to look for these signals in others to determine if they are truthful, we must check in with our own body language because we may inadvertently signal that we should not be trusted.

In the body language world, there is a saying: "Move the body, move the mind." Just by changing our posture, we can change our mindset. If you haven't seen Amy Cuddy's TED talk about power poses, you should. She proved through cortisol levels present in saliva swabs that when we stand tall like Superman, we can change our brain's chemistry and suppress cortisol. The more space our bodies take up, the more confident we feel. Most of us ball up when we feel any sense of insecurity or worry. Our shoulders slump and curl forward; we slouch, drop our head, and tuck our chin. We become smaller. These postures indicate closed body language, and others can perceive us as uncomfortable and untrustworthy. How will you gain someone's trust if you look untrustworthy? You must maintain open body language to look and feel confident.

Here is a checklist of what your body language should be doing to gain interest and trust from others:

- *Keep your body language open.* That means do not cover your neck, belly button, or groin. We call these three areas "power zones" because we unintentionally cover them up when we feel fear. When our amygdala senses fear, such as the fear of telling the truth, we tend to guard these three vital areas of the body that protect vital organs. Look for when others cover up these areas because it is a sign they sense fear. Be mindful of when you cover up these areas because it can send the signal you can't be trusted.
- *Keep your arms uncrossed.* Even though people cross their arms out of comfort and right before making a big decision, it is commonly perceived as a defensive posture. So, get into the habit of keeping your arms unfolded and by your side.
- *Maintain reciprocal eye contact.* Do not stare a person down because that may be perceived as aggressive. Look at them as they prefer to look at you. You may be speaking to a person who does not feel comfortable with direct eye contact. If you give them too much, you will increase their anxiety. And if you do that, you could mistake that anxiety as deceptive behavior.

- *Align with them*. Keep your belly button and feet aligned with those of your POI. It sends the signal you are interested in them. Once you lean back and angle your torso somewhere else, it can signal that you have lost interest in them. This is also true for your POI. If they suddenly shift their angle and move their torso and feet to point to a door, they probably want to leave.

- *Avoid self-pacifying gestures.* When some people become nervous or feel insecure, they will begin to preen themselves. They may rub their hands, arms, and legs. Or they may pick their fingernails, play with their rings, or tug at their clothing. They may even caress their upper lip with their finger. People tend to do this as a way to console themselves when they are feeling uncomfortable. If you observe yourself doing this, bring your hands back to the table or down by your side.

SEEK FIRST TO DETECT THE TRUTH

First and foremost, here is what you need to know when detecting deception and especially when analyzing nonverbal behaviors: you must always work just as hard to detect the truth. If you do not, you may never see deception, or you may see deception in truthful people. Anyone can learn how to read body language, but I teach others how to objectively assess nonverbal behaviors and differentiate between natural stress and stress from lying. You will see physiological responses to stress in people because the atmosphere is tense. You will see those same responses in people who are lying. But not all liars experience anxiety when they lie.

When I conduct deceptive analysis, both verbally and nonverbally, I note both truthful and deceptive displays. In fact, when I am baselining an individual both during the rapport phase at the beginning of the interview and throughout the interview, I write "NV" for nonverbal and "V" for verbal on my notepad, and I fill in the behaviors I notice under each. I count and compare them. And when someone asks why I think they are telling the truth I can say, "Because there were seven indicators of truth-telling," instead of saying, "I didn't observe any deceptive indicators."

To be good at detecting deception, you have to be good at detecting the truth. There will be times where you will see and hear deceptive as well as truthful indicators, but if you know what to look and listen for, you can determine which one outweighs the other. As I go through all of the nonverbal indicators of deception I have laid out in this chapter, I will also be telling you the flip side of the indicator, which is indicative of truth-telling.

First, I want to talk about the science behind lying so you understand why a truthful person can look deceitful and why a liar can look confident and even pass a polygraph test.

LIE DETECTORS

Before I get into lie detectors (and by the way, there is no such thing as a lie detector), I want to discuss the nervous system and our memories. Think of the nervous system as a call center where messages are constantly coming in and out. The nervous system is divided into the central nervous system and the peripheral nervous system. The central nervous system includes the brain and spinal cord. We are going to concentrate on the brain. You are already familiar with the limbic system from chapter 8, but I will dissect it further.

The limbic system is responsible for our emotions, motivations, survival instincts, and memories. Because it reacts to stimuli in real time, it is called the honest brain, even when you experience an irrational explosion of anger. The limbic system is why most of us respond to lying with anxiety. I must warn you, though, there are people out there who do not feel anxiety when they lie. According to an article by science journalist Ronald Kotulak, "With brain imaging technology, they can see how a lie sparks activity deep in the limbic system, the center of emotion and self-preservation. The lie gathers support from the memory banks in the left and right temporal lobes and then makes a dash to the frontal cortex, where a decision is made to suppress what the brain knows to be true."

Or, as my friend Elly Johnson, a former Australian police officer, says, lying is a choice; first, you must suppress the truth.

Most people believe a polygraph machine can detect lies, but it can't. It can only detect physiological responses to stress. There are two types of liars: regular and powerful. A "regular" liar worries about creating the lie, keeping the lie up, and getting caught in the lie. That describes most of us. As a result, we become so nervous that we may experience cognitive overload. The other type of liar is called a "powerful" liar. No, they are not good at lying. It's simply that they are not concentrating on worry, but on the reward of the lie. If they lie on their resume, for example, they are more focused on getting the job than on getting caught. Because they are not worried about lying, they do not experience stress, and therefore their stress response system does not kick into gear. Many people ask me if it is possible to catch a powerful liar when they are lying. The answer is yes. If they do not leak any nonverbal indicators of deception, they certainly will when they speak. You will learn more about this in the next chapter.

To use a polygraph as a lie detector is to assume that everyone who lies will experience stress and anxiety. Not everyone does. That's why US spies such as Ana Montes, Aldrich Ames, and Robert Hanssen all sold secrets to foreign governments and passed their polygraph exams every year. They were powerful liars who were focused on the reward of the lie.

The only machine that can accurately detect a lie is a functional MRI scan that can see the brain activity associated with lying and truth-telling. The bottom line is that when a person does not like to lie, the limbic system responds to their lie with anxiety, which is good for human lie detectors to observe. The stress will also cause cognitive overload and the lie will start to unravel quickly.

I often get asked about sociopaths and pathological liars. Pathological liars lie to manipulate and deceive others without any regret, guilt, or shame. They tend to have big egos and become agitated when confronted with lying. Compulsive liars, or habitual liars, lie for no reason. They do not do it for personal gain, and there is no clear motivation as to why they lie. Either can be easily proven wrong but will continue to lie even when they know you know they are lying.

Scientists say that the brain can adapt to dishonesty; the more dishonest we become, the easier it is to be dishonest. From the constant embellisher to the pathological liar, the limbic system becomes desensitized to the anxiety of lying, and we feel less anxious when we lie. Now that you know this, please do not start to lie compulsively in hopes that you can get away with a lie. Even when people begin to be okay with lying and the reactionary emotional response is less anxiety, the truth always leaks out.

HOW WE CREATE LIES FROM MEMORY

Inside the limbic system is the hippocampus, which is primarily responsible for our memory. It consolidates information from short-term to long-term memory. There are two types of memories: episodic and semantic. Episodic memories are autobiographical; they are created from actual real-life experiences. They consist of things we have done, places we have been, people we have met, sights and sounds we have experienced, and emotions we have felt. We store our autobiographical memories as discrete pieces of information. So when we go to retrieve these memories, we have to piece together the bits of information and re-create the event. Think of what you did last night. To yourself, recite out loud what you did. You probably will do this in

150

a timeline sequence rather than a story. Now, if I ask you to do the same thing next week, next month, or next year, each time you have to recall what you did last night, you will still be piecing together the separate bits of information to make a complete story. The problem is that a year from now, some of those bits of information will have dropped off in your memory bank. You will not be able to retrieve them because you forgot them. As time goes on, it requires more work to piece together our actual, autobiographical events. I bet you are beginning to see an issue when it comes to detecting deception. If I question a POI about an actual event that happened months ago, it will be harder for them to recall the bits of episodic memory than if I were asking what they did last night. As a deceptive analysis expert, I have to make sure I do not jump the gun and assume their difficulty recalling events is deception.

Semantic memories are remembrances that we have processed from ideas and concepts that are common knowledge to us and not from our personal experiences. We have collected these bits of information over time just from being human and living on this earth. You all probably know what a space shuttle is even though you have likely never been in one or seen one in real life. When detecting deception, the difficulty comes with trying to discern between people's semantic memories (not personally experienced) and episodic memories (personally experienced). When people lie, they use their semantic memory to create an untruthful story or event. For example, I could lie to you and tell you that I have been to Kennedy Space Center in Florida and watched a space shuttle launch. I could even describe a visual picture of it to prove my story. But in reality, I am using bits of semantic memory from what I have seen on TV because I have never been to Kennedy Space Center. Now you may be thinking, "Well, shoot, how am I going to tell if someone is lying to me using a created event from semantic memory?"

Easy. Keep reading.

COGNITIVE OVERLOAD

Thankfully, both types of liars can reach cognitive overload. "Cognitive load" is the total amount of mental effort used in the working memory, the part of our brain constantly processing information. Working memory creates memory schemas that get transferred to long-term memory. We pull these memory schemas from our long-term memory to our working memory to help us understand things. If we could not do this, we would not remember what a stop sign means, and I would not be able to write this book without looking at the keyboard.

Now let's talk about the cognitive process used to create lies. You know that we have to retrieve memories, even truthful ones, and put them together to tell a story. That takes mental effort, especially when you start asking about dates, times, and specific information that truthful people may be struggling to retrieve. Liars retrieve memories as well. And they can experience cognitive overload when their working memory gets overburdened trying to bring semantic memories forward to create a fabrication.

When someone is experiencing cognitive overload, they cannot handle normal thinking processes:

- They mix up details or forget them altogether.
- Their speech slows down, and they say less.
- They use smaller, simpler words.
- Their sentences become shorter.
- Feelings and emotions that should be attached to the story they are telling become nonexistent (except for stress and anxiety).
- They do not even hear you when you ask a question; their attention goes inward instead of outward, and they appear to "zone out."
- Some may even become physically ill from the stress.

If a person you are interviewing has reached cognitive overload, they will not have the mental capacity to keep up their lie. It will begin to unravel fast, and then they will reach the breaking point.

GETTING THE BASELINE

Now that you understand the two types of liars and how lies are created, you are ready to baseline, a critical tool for detecting deception. What does a baseline do? It allows you to get an accurate read on how a person prefers to behave when relaxed. A person's relaxed behavioral patterns will change when they become stressed and when they lie.

The best way to get an accurate baseline on a person's overall demeanor is to get them relaxed and comfortable. Baselining typically happens during the rapport phase of an interview. You talk about their hobbies, their family, or what's going on in the news. Sometimes you may just have to sit back and listen to them talk about whatever they want. During this time, you can baseline how a person looks and sounds. Here is what to look for in a POI's nonverbal communication:

- Are they fidgety or still?
- Do they give or avoid direct eye contact?
- Do they tap their feet or fingers?
- Do they make facial expressions and raise their eyebrows often?
- Are they incongruent with their head nods and shakes (do they always shake their head "no" even when saying "yes")?
- Are they excitable and energetic or relaxed and calm?
- Do they have good posture or do they slouch?
- Do they use self-pacifying gestures?
- Where do their eyes anchor when retrieving episodic memories vs. semantic memories?

And here is what to listen for when baselining how they sound:

- What is their rate of speech? Do they naturally speak fast or slow?
- What is the pitch of their voice? Typically, when a person lies, the pitch of their voice rises because of the stress on their vocal cords.
- What is their tone of voice? Is it sarcastic, formal, friendly, positive, or negative?
- What is the volume of their voice? Does this person tend to speak softly?
- Do they hesitate frequently, and if so, what is the duration and frequency of their pauses?
- Do they use filler words such as "um" and "uh"?
- Do they tend to tongue smack? Listen for people smack their tongue; it can be a hesitation or stalling tactic when thinking of what to say. It buys a few seconds to choose words wisely.
- What types of words and phrases do they use? I call these "pet words." Some people always hedge what they are going to say with, "You are never going to believe this . . ." while others preface anything they say with the word "so." These can be indicators of deception, but not for people who say these phrases as their baseline.

During the baseline, you must consider contextual circumstances, meaning the context of the surrounding environment. A person may be nervous because they are about to be interviewed or polygraphed. We need to determine whether they are worried and nervous about the interview or if they are lying. There is an easy way to tell the difference.

ARE YOU STRESSED OR LYING?

When people are under tremendous amounts of stress, their mouths and eyes can become dry. As a result, they will have a difficult time swallowing and even speaking because there is no saliva, and they may rapidly blink their eyes in an effort to lubricate them. Outside of dry eye syndrome or an issue with a contact lens, I have noticed that the blink rate increases when people lie.

When a person reaches the fight-or-flight state and cortisol is released, blood and oxygen are surging through the body, and the skin on the face and neck can become itchy. Because our heads do not have muscles like our arms and legs, the blood gets closer to the skin's surface, which in turn can create an itchy sensation. People will tend to swipe their tear lines or touch their noses during stress. When I teach my classes, I show them videos of known liars such as Lance Armstrong, Anthony Weiner, Jodi Arias, and Chris Watts. They all touched their faces when they spoke because they were stressed from lying. But what if you are unsure if someone is being dishonest? How can you decipher if the stress indicators you see are a result of lying? There is a simple way to answer that question. If you see and hear indicators of deception, they are lying. The most accurate indicator of deception is behavioral incongruence.

THE MOST ACCURATE
INDICATOR OF DECEPTION

Behavioral incongruence is when our body language does not match our spoken language. I will give you some examples.

INCONGRUENT SHOULDER SHRUGS

Let's say your POI tells you they have no idea why a person would say
they were responsible for a crime. As the POI says this, they shrug
their shoulders. A shoulder shrug always means uncertainty. If a person says, "I have no idea," while shrugging their shoulders, they are
congruent. Their words and the shoulder shrug are both expressing
uncertainty. Now, if someone says, "I know exactly what happened,"
and they shrug their shoulders, you have a problem. They are doubt-
ing what they are saying. And so should you.

INCONGRUENT OPENNESS

Suppose someone says, "I'd be open to talking about that with you,"
and as they say this, they cross their arms and ankles and lean back.
Those three movements say they are not open to talking because they
just closed up their body. If this person felt open to discussing a sensitive matter with you, they would have opened their stance.

We can open and close our hands as well as our posture. When we
speak with our hands and show our palms, that can signify we are
open and truthful. When we hide the palms of our hands or face them
inward toward the body, that can tell someone that we are not open
and therefore dishonest.

INCONGRUENT HEAD NODS AND SHAKES

In most cultures, head-nodding signifies "yes," and head shaking signifies "no." If someone says, "I like that idea," but is shaking their head
sideways, they may not like that idea. There is a 2010 *Dateline Special*
interview between Matt Lauer and Britney Spears where Lauer says
to Spears, "When the magazine screams on the cover, pregnant and
divorcing—" Britney cuts him off. "No, none of that's true," she says as
she is nodding yes. She also leaks some incongruent facial expressions

of emotions such as sincere sadness (her bottom lip is protruding while the corners of her mouth arch downward and her eyes close), contempt (which I will talk about shortly), and anger. If this was indeed not true, why is she incongruent with her head nods and her emotions? (You can see this video on YouTube: https://www.youtube.com/watch?v=XPbqNReDETo.)

INCONGRUENT EMOTIONS

Psychologist Paul Ekman is the pioneer when it comes to facial expressions of emotions. He has proven that they are universal and that there is a difference between how truth, embellishment, and deception appear on people's faces. An embellished emotion, which is a dishonest emotion, lasts on the face longer than a true emotion. When people are trying to mask their true emotion to deceive us, it flashes across the face for less than a second according to Ekman. He refers to this as a "micro-expression." You have to pay close attention in order to see it, however. We must be able to decipher the emotion we see. Is it embellished? For example, if someone tells you they like your idea, but as they say this they leak disgust (crinkling at the bridge of the nose and/or curling the upper lip), that should tell you they detest your idea. If someone tells you they understand why you made a certain decision, but they show doubt (furrowed eyebrows or raised, squinting eyes, eye gaze up or to the side, head tilt to one side, or lips pursed), they may not understand or agree with your decision.

I want to focus on one particular emotion Ekman calls contempt, which I mentioned earlier. Contempt means moral superiority. People show contempt (a half-smile or smirk) when they feel they are better than someone, think they have the upper hand, know they are admired, and believe they have gotten away with a lie. In my many years of interviewing POIs and analyzing videos, I have learned that most people will leak contempt after they lie.

Many of you will recognize the name Chris Watts. On August 13, 2018, he killed his wife, Shanann, and his two young daughters, Bella and Celeste. He was arrested two days later and charged with three counts of first-degree murder. He is currently serving five life sentences. The day his family disappeared, Shanann's friend called the police. Bodycam footage captured the police interview that day. Immediately, I knew Watts was lying. He was smiling and showing contempt during most of the interview and shrugging his shoulders and shaking his head "no." A little more than one minute in, the police officer asks Watts what the names of his kids are. He responds, "Bella and Celeste," then he does a prolonged eyeblink and leaks contempt. A prolonged eyeblink can indicate that a person is trying to visualize something or block out an emotion. It can also mean that they are experiencing a negative emotion. And it can happen right before a person tries to deceive you. In my opinion, Watts's show of contempt indicates that he knows something about his daughters that we don't, and he did; he knew he had killed them.

You also should take notice of when a person's tongue protrudes. You may remember when you were young sticking out your tongue to your siblings. Adults do the same thing, just not so obvious. When people are angry and feeling discomfort, they will purse their lips. Not only will our lips disappear when we experience anger, but our tongues will appear when we don't like something. The tongue show is a universal mood sign of unspoken disagreement, disbelief, disliking, and displeasure. If you see someone's tongue come out and it is not because they are licking their lips to lubricate the mouth, they may be telling you they don't like you or what you are saying.

CONVINCING BODY LANGUAGE OF LIARS

I have a saying: *Liars convince, truth-tellers convey.* In the next chapter, you will learn about convincing language; now, you will understand how they use their body language to convince you of a lie.

Liars will try to convince you of what they are saying by pointing their fingers as they are talking. You saw Bill Clinton do this when he said on tape, "I did not have sexual relations with that woman, Miss Lewinsky." Also, as he said this, his rate of speech slowed down dramatically, another convincing technique. When a person becomes hostile or defensive as a result of lying, they will typically begin to point as they talk to try to bully you into believing them.

Another convincing nonverbal action is when people display "praying hands," also called pleading or mercy hands. This is when their palms are turned upward in a plea gesture as though they are saying, "Please believe me!" This could be sincere, but if other convincing gestures or deceptive indicators accompany it, it probably means that person is trying to get you to believe their lie.

Hands with palms pressed together indicate a more anxious pleading. This gesture may be made with fingers upward in a clear prayer position ("Please do not harm me!") and possibly thrust toward you.

Some liars know that the eyes can give away their secret, so instead of looking away, as some people do because they don't want to face you when they lie, they will glare at you without breaking eye contact. This forced eye contact is not natural.

THE BOTTOM LINE

Accurately analyzing body language is difficult and requires awareness. There are many nonverbal gestures and movements that can indicate deception but may also be displayed by a person telling the truth. Use my rule of three: first, baseline a person's overall demeanor;

second, look for multiple signs of deception; and third, consider the context of the situation and environment. People get nervous in interviews even when they are telling the truth. Do not jump the gun and assume deception if you see signs of anxiety and stress. You have to see indicators of deception. Look for behavioral incongruence to identify when a person is deceitful.

I'll end this chapter with an experience I had during a trip to Washington, DC, when teaching at the Body Language Institute with Janine Driver in her week-long, intensive, train-the-trainer class. On my last day there, one of the attendees, Rob, told his stories (one true, the other not) in the hot seat. I was half paying attention to him and half trying to figure out something on my laptop. The rest of the class asked him nonpertinent questions to get his baseline verbal and nonverbal behavior. After a few minutes of making Rob feel relaxed, the facilitator asked him to tell his stories. As I was listening to Rob and glancing up here and there to observe him, I picked up on a few things immediately that made me believe his second story was his lie. As he began to tell it, his speech rate dropped dramatically from his baseline and from his first story. His voice also became softer. So much so I looked up to pay more attention to him. As I did, he began to leak disgust. He appeared to be experiencing negative emotions, but the story was supposed to be joyful. He hardly moved his arms, which was completely different from when he told his first story. And finally, he said something that convinced me he was lying: "I wanted to make it to the NBA. That's everyone's dream." If it was *his* dream, he should have said that, but he didn't. I had to validate my decision, so I took over the questioning. When I asked him about his first story (the truthful one), he took notice that I doubted the validity of that story, and he began to leak contempt when he answered me. Usually, contempt signifies deception, but in this case, it made perfect sense that I saw it when he was telling the truth. He thought he had tricked me! And because of that, he thought he was getting one over on me. The first story, by the way, had to do with him being in a commercial with Michael Jordan and Kevin Bacon. Who is going to believe that? The class was divided in half on which story they thought was his lie. When they asked me to answer, I stuck with the initial choice. Even though being in a commercial with Michael Jordan and Kevin Bacon seemed doubtful, the second story had more deceptive indicators. And I was right.

Even though I may begin to doubt myself at times, I always come back to two things. One, do not second-guess yourself. Two, believe in the science behind detecting deception.

• • •

"Look for the marriage between the body language and words; they will not be in sync if one is cheating."

—LENA SISCO

ACTIVITY

Watch this video of Chris Watts, liar and murderer, on YouTube: https://www.youtube.com/watch?v=ugoYkx04E2Q.

Watch until 1 minute, 35 seconds and write down all the nonverbal signs of stress and deception. The answers are in Appendix C.

12

DECEPTIVE STATEMENTS AND ANSWERS

HAVE YOU EVER heard that communication is 93 percent nonverbal and 7 percent verbal? Do you agree? If you are like most people, you would have said, "Yes." Let me give you a little history lesson on the origin of this statement, which may shock you. In 1971, psychologist Albert Mehrabian did indeed prove that those numbers are accurate in a study he conducted on communication. However, his experiment was not meant for all communication contexts, and as such his data is often misinterpreted.

According to ChangingMinds.org's summation of his experiment:

He had subjects listen to nine recorded words, three conveying liking (honey, dear and thanks), three conveying neutrality (maybe, really and oh) and three conveying disliking (don't, brute and terrible). The words were spoken using different tonalities and said with different facial expressions. The listeners were asked to identify the emotion the speaker was demonstrating by listening to the speaker's tone of voice and seeing the speaker's facial expressions. His experiment found that tone of voice carried more meaning than the individual words themselves in the message, and that facial expressions more accurately depicted the emotion for the viewers, than the tone of voice or words, in the delivery of the message. So therefore, he concluded that communication was in three parts, words, which accounted for 7 percent, voice tone, which accounted for 38 percent, and facial expressions, which accounted for 55 percent. Combining voice tone and facial expressions you get 93 percent which he stated signified nonverbal communication. His findings actually proved nonverbal communication took primacy in the delivery of a message. However, only within a certain communication context was this true. In fact, in "Silent Messages" he writes this: "Please note that this and other equations regarding relative importance of verbal and nonverbal messages were derived from experiments dealing with communications of feelings and attitudes (i.e., like-dislike). Unless a communicator is talking about their feelings or attitudes, these equations are not applicable."

Since this is the only statistical research study conducted on verbal vs. nonverbal communication measures, people incorrectly assume that humans communicate 93 percent nonverbally and 7 percent verbally in all communication contexts. Because of this flawed use of his analysis, many people think that when they detect deception in others, they will see more deceptive indicators in a person's nonverbal body language than in their verbal language. Thus, when looking for deceptive indicators, people may put more emphasis on analyzing body language than spoken language.

Since this book is about getting honest answers, you need to know when someone isn't truthful and when they are honest. Because the focus of this book is on interviewing and negotiating, I will give you

real-world examples of interview responses and dissect them to re-
veal hidden messages. I can almost guarantee you have heard these
responses before, or you will hear them, because all liars tend to
sound alike. After reading this chapter, I am confident that you will be
able to conduct statement analysis like a pro. Statement analysis is a
term coined by Mark McClish, a former Secret Service agent who
founded a company called Advanced Interviewing Concepts. In 2020,
I had the opportunity to appear on Eric Hunley's *Unstructured* podcast with Mark, who was doing statement analysis long before me. I
also interviewed Mark for this book so I could share some of his expertise with you.

In this chapter, you will learn how a liar sounds and how they tend
to respond to questions that they don't want to answer. I will discuss
the eight deceptive languages that liars use, including formalizing
(something I discovered and coined in my research study), minimizing, distancing, convincing, softening, assuming, noncommittal, and
storytelling. I will also cover these common verbal indicators of deception: fluff (my own terminology for when someone is talking to
appear open and cooperative, but they are not telling you anything of
importance), unnecessary words, repetition, missing personal pronouns, and the use of the passive voice.

During the COVID pandemic, I started the Profiler Task Force with
three other women, all of whom are experts in human behavior.
Together, we were the leading authorities in body language, handwriting analysis, and interrogation. As the interrogator, my part was
to analyze statements for truth and deception. I started referring to
myself as a "word nerd" because I love to pick them apart to discover
hidden meanings. So I will begin with the importance of words.

People use words on purpose, but they may do so unconsciously.
What I mean is that the speaker will usually leak the truth. Jerry
Sandusky, former Penn State University assistant coach and convicted sex offender, is a good example. In 2013, before he was convicted of sexual abuse and sent to prison, Sandusky was interviewed

by Jo Becker of the *New York Times*. During this interview, Becker asked him what restrictions Tim Curley, former Penn State athletic director, put on him after hearing about the pedophilia allegations made against him. Sandusky answered: "I was told I couldn't work them out anymore, so I asked, well, can I just work them out?" Obviously, Jerry has two meanings for "work them out." He used the word "just" right before "work them out." "Just" is a minimizing word, which means he was minimizing what he was about to say next, which was "work them out." So, did the first version of "work them out" mean to abuse them sexually, and the second version, which he minimized, stand for innocently working them out with calisthenics? We don't know for sure, but there is a reason why Sandusky did not change the words in his statement. My opinion is because he viewed sexual abuse and calisthenics as the same thing, with neither being illegal or immoral.

Remember, we choose our words consciously and unconsciously, and usually, the truth will slip out unconsciously. For example, say you are interviewing a suspect who you believe is part of a human trafficking ring. During questioning about human smuggling operations across the border, he tells you, "I would never smuggle kids across the border, that's child slavery, and I would never do that to kids. I have kids of my own, and I protect them!" First, he said that he "would never" smuggle children, not that he hasn't. He also doesn't say anything about smuggling adults. He may think of illegally bringing children across the border not as "smuggling" but "protecting" them from their life in their home country. As an interviewer, you would need to question this subject on how he "protects" kids and smuggles adults.

I bet now you are beginning to understand why I believe words are the most crucial element in detecting deception. People tend to want to control their body language when they lie because they think that is what people like me are looking for. However, most people do not control their words when they lie, and their words will dime them out every time. Matching someone's body language with their spoken language is vital to identify behavioral incongruency, which in my opinion, is the most accurate indicator of deception.

A LIAR'S TENDENCIES

As you are aware from the previous chapter, when people have to remember a rehearsed lie or when they have to come up with a lie on the fly, they can experience cognitive overload from the increase in mental effort. So when you ask questions to someone who doesn't want to answer with the truth, or chooses to answer with a lie, there are deceptive tendencies for both, and they have to do with cognitive overload. First, let me remind you that when a liar decides to lie and then has to suppress the truth, it is a choice. The truth is always there, and it will take work to keep it from leaking out. Sometimes the truth is embedded in a sentence or a phrase, and other times it is replaced by another word.

In order for you to be able to decipher an honest answer from a deceptive one, I will explain the typical responses liars give when creating false statements and when they are lying by omission.

MISPLACED EMOTIONS

You know from chapter 5 that I have four lie exposing questions. One is, "How did that make you feel?" A truthful person will tell you how they felt and a deceptive person will have to think of how they should have felt. You will hear the difference in their answers. But emotions can identify deception in another way as well. An indicator of deception not only happens when someone forgets to attach feelings and emotions in a story, but it can also happen when a person puts them in the wrong place. In truthful accounts, people will express emotions after the event, not during. When emotions are included in the dramatic part of the story, it is indicative of storytelling. Here is an example: "I hurriedly ran downstairs" (deceptive) vs. "I ran downstairs in a hurry" (truthful).

WHEN THEY TELL YOU WHAT THEY DIDN'T DO

I once read part of a witness statement by a man who murdered his baby boy by shaking him too hard because he wouldn't stop crying. In his statement, he wrote, "I tried to stop him from crying. I picked him up. He was fussing and screaming. I was trying to control him, and then he squirmed out of my arms. That's when his body fell headfirst to the ground." Let's analyze this statement, which is full of deception. First, as you can see, he wrote that he tried to stop the baby from crying. That most likely means the baby didn't stop crying. I'm okay with that statement because he goes on to tell the authorities that the baby was fussing and screaming. That backs up his earlier statement, and we know the baby is still crying. Then he writes, "I was trying to control him, and then he squirmed out of my arms." Here we have a problem. Since he again uses "trying," we can deduce he wasn't able to control his son. My question is, what exactly was he trying to control? The crying or something else? And here is when the truth leaks out. He writes, "That's when his body fell headfirst to the ground." Does anything sound strange to you? The fact that he wrote "his body" instead of the baby's name tells me that the baby was already dead or unresponsive. Working on homicide cases, I have observed that the moment a person knows that another person is deceased, they refer to the deceased as an inanimate object. It turned out that this guy shook his baby so hard to get him to stop crying that he caused severe brain damage, and he tried to cover it up by faking a head injury from falling.

In the example I gave earlier, when someone tells us they "would never" do something, they are not telling us they didn't do it. If a person tells us they "had to do" something, that doesn't tell us they did it.

My niece told me her new boyfriend decided to break up with his old girlfriend. I told her to dump him. "He may have decided to break up with his old girlfriend," I told her, "but he may not have actually broken up with her. He may be dating both of you." I happened to be right (she dumped him the following week). So, when someone tells you they "decided" to do something, they are saying they decided, and that is it. The same goes for the words "started" and "attempted." Both of these words indicate intention but not completion.

The words, "tried," "wanted," "decided," "started," "attempted," "began," and "would" all indicate talk of an action and intention of an action. But in reality, the action never happened.

THE SETUP WORDS

Liars as well as truth-tellers use "setup" words like "so" and "well." These words are preparatory commands for heavy content to come. It may be a lie such as a rehearsed part of a story. It may be something we aren't expecting, like constructive feedback, or it may be something emotional. Whatever it is, it is a mild warning for what is about to be said. However, these words can also be "pet words" that people say all the time. I for one say "So . . ." frequently. Because of that, I will reiterate the importance of baselining a person's speech patterns in order to avoid incorrectly assessing deception in truthful people. Both "well" and "so" can be used as stalling tactics to buy a person some time to digest what someone has said to them, or to think of what to say back—which could be the truth or a lie.

In a 2010 *Psychology Today* article, author, psychologist, retired FBI agent, and professor Jack Schaffer, PhD, wrote, "If you begin a sentence with 'well' there is a good chance you are lying," because it indicates that the person is about to give you an answer you aren't expecting. According to Schaffer, it only works with yes-or-no questions.

TOO MANY GENERALIZATIONS

To avoid details and giving specifics, liars tend to generalize and use words such as "always," "never," "sometimes," and "all the time." If the person you are questioning should know details about an event due to their job, status, role, relationship, or involvement, and they use generalizations, that indicates that they do not want to share specifics with you.

Say you are attending a trade show. You meet your competitor, and you start a conversation. To avoid giving away proprietary information, your competitor may use generalizations. You ask them, "Have you encountered any problems with the new software?" They respond with, "The usual first-line glitches." If you are questioning a character witness on behalf of a mother fighting for custody of her child, you ask her, "Describe some instances when Lucy has demonstrated positive character traits with regard to raising her child." Your character witness says, "Lucy is a great mom and a great mother figure. She loves her daughter more than anything." This doesn't differentiate Lucy from any other mother out there. You need to hear specific instances that the character witness has actually observed.

In sales, generalizations can cause you to lose clients. Prospects may think you are being evasive because you lack experience. You can lose a person's trust if you don't show confidence in what you say. If you lack confidence, you may lose your buyer's confidence in you. Give exact figures, numbers, and statistics and stand by them.

THEY REFUSE TO ANSWER THE QUESTION

When ABC's Barbara Pinto asked Drew Peterson about his missing wife, Stacy, during one of many interviews he gave before his arrest in 2009, she said, "Do you think [Stacy] is the kind of person who would just take off and leave her children?" Drew does not answer her. Instead, he avoids answering the question by saying, "Do you ever really know someone?" People who have something to hide will answer a question with a question, repeat the question back, or ask why you are asking that question. If I were Drew's interviewer, I would have fired back, "Why would Stacy just take off and leave her children?" I give my POIs three chances to answer, and if they strike out on the third try, I confront them by asking calmly, "I have asked you the same question three times. Is there any reason why you won't answer my question?" Then I wait for them to respond.

EIGHT DECEPTIVE LANGUAGES

There are eight deceptive languages that liars tend to use—almost always unwittingly: formalizing, minimizing, distancing, convincing, softening, assuming, noncommittal, and storytelling.

FORMALIZING

I discovered this verbal indicator of deception in 2015, when I trained over six hundred Customs and Border Patrol agents. In an exercise, students would sit in front of the class and tell two stories: a truthful one and a lie. The challenge was for the class to determine which one was the lie. I noticed that when the students lied, they would use the word "recall" instead of "remember." When they were telling the truth, they would usually say, "I don't remember" instead of "I don't recollect." They would also use other forms of formal language such as "place of employment" instead of "work" and "compensated" instead of "paid." To me it sounded like they were trying to oversell their lie by sounding more formal.

According to Oxford Dictionary, "formal" means, "Done in accordance with rules of convention or etiquette." When liars lie, they try to convince you to believe their lie. A way to do that is to oversell what they are saying by formalizing it. They try to make you assume they are following "rules of convention" and telling the truth. It's almost as though liars think you have to believe them because they speak well. They think if they sound educated, then they must sound believable.

Be sure you baseline a person's verbal speech patterns first because some people and professions tend to use formal words when they are being truthful. For example, everyone I have ever met in law enforcement uses the word "recall." It is part of their vocabulary.

MINIMIZING

Minimizing language reduces the significance of what is being said. The easiest way to identify minimizing language is by the use of two words: "just" and "only." When people minimize their actions using the word "just," it indicates that they may have done more than what they are telling you. For example, if your coworker took a longer than usual lunch break and they tell you, "I just went to McDonald's and came back," there is a chance they minimized what they really did. Perhaps they didn't *just* go to McDonald's.

When people use the word "only," they are also minimizing or downplaying what they are talking about. That doesn't mean that people who say "just" and "only" are lying, but it can mean they are lying by omitting information. It can also mean they don't want to get into an argument, so they are telling you up front "it's not a big deal." Here is an example of minimizing language you may hear during an internal audit regarding loss prevention: You are part of the audit team, and you are interviewing an employee with a known criminal record. You ask her, "Why did you open the boxes of new inventory before checking in with your manager?" She answers, "I just only wanted to make sure we got the right delivery." Now, I am not saying this employee is lying, but she did use minimizing language, so it is your responsibility to find out what she minimized and why. Could it be she suspects you think she is lying so she is letting you know she didn't have a nefarious reason for opening them? Or could it be she opened them for another reason she is concealing?

DISTANCING

Liars will try to distance themselves from the lie, or the person, thing, or event that is associated with the lie. As you have already read, most people feel uncomfortable lying, and being deceitful can cause stress, anxiety, worry, guilt, and shame. So when a person lies, they tend to use language that disassociates them from the lie. For example, when former president Bill Clinton referred to Monica Lewinsky as "that woman" in his infamous speech ("I did not have sexual relations with that woman . . ."), he wanted to get away from being associated with her. From years of interviewing and assisting law enforcement in criminal cases, I have found when a person refers to a person they have killed, or they know has been killed, they talk about the person in the past tense. I'll return to the still-unsolved death of JonBenet Ramsey as an example. In 1996, Patsy Ramsey made a phone call to 911 the morning she claims to have realized JonBenet went missing. According to a recording of this phone call, the 911 operator says, "Okay, what's your name? Are you—" Patsy cuts her off and says, "Patsy Ramsey, I'm the mother." "*The* mother?" Why not "I'm *her* mother?" This is a classic example of distancing language. Now that Patsy knows her daughter isn't coming back to life, and she has guilty knowledge of her murder (at least I believe she did), she wants to distance herself from the crime and from the victim of the crime.

The articles "a" and "the" can tell a lot more than you think. Another example of distancing language has to do with definite and indefinite articles.

The definite article "the" is used before a person, place, or thing, when it is a known thing. When someone uses the indefinite article "a" it means the noun is unknown. For example, if during an interview your POI says, "He pointed *the* gun at me," that means the person telling you this has either introduced the gun before in the story or knows about the gun. If they say, "He pointed *a* gun at me," that tells you the gun is unknown or hasn't been introduced yet by the POI. The problem comes when the POI hasn't introduced or spoken about a person, let's say, but refers to the person as a known entity. Let's pretend you are a detective questioning a burglary victim. The victim is the husband, and he claims that someone broke into his home, held him at gunpoint, and stole his wife's expensive jewelry. If he says, "A man broke into my home, held me at gunpoint, and stole my wife's jewelry," he could be telling the truth. If he says, "The man broke into my home, held me at gunpoint, and stole my wife's jewelry," he knows this man. (It is not uncommon for people to do this to collect insurance money.)

Once a person or thing has been introduced, we should be using "the." "I was standing at the bus stop when a man approached me and asked me what time it was. The man then pointed the gun at me and told me to give him my wallet." Here, the storyteller introduces "*a* man," and after that he is required to use "*the* man." This does not indicate deception; it is following the rules of grammar. If, however, a person refuses to use "the" on a known entity, that is indicative of distancing language.

Drew Peterson gives a great example of distancing in this 2008 interview with the late Larry King: https://www.youtube.com/watch?v=c_PRGT8N8YE. During this interview regarding the disappearance of his wife, Drew states: "You know I'm a police officer and I don't work for the phone company or the power company and as a police officer we don't have the same ability to do things as the common person. If I get involved in a domestic situation where I'm physical with a wife, I'll lose my job." First, I bet you didn't know that those of you who work for a phone company or power company have the "ability" to get involved in a domestic situation? Remember what I said earlier in this chapter: words have meaning. Why would Drew say something like that? In all seriousness, he does say, "*a* wife," not "*my*

wife," or "*the* wife." Perhaps he is talking about his past wives or potential future wives. Either way, it sounds odd. Why would he distance
himself from the word "wife," especially when the entire interview
was about his current wife's disappearance?

I've heard people talk about their spouses as "the wife" or "the husband" and their marriage as "the marriage." It tells me they want
some distance, possibly emotional or physical, from their spouse or
marriage. If you are dating someone and they refer to your relationship as "the relationship," you need to have a discussion; they may
want to distance themselves from you. People like to create distance
between themselves and things that make them feel uncomfortable.

CONVINCING

Deceptive people try to *convince* us of information. Truthful people
convey information. I've already mentioned that convincing tactics
can come nonverbally and verbally. Nonverbally, a person may use
their body to become bigger and take up more space. They may point
their index finger at you when speaking; they may increase their eye
contact so much that they glare at you. All signs they are trying to convince you to believe what they are verbally selling you. Sometimes
deceptive people will make convincing statements to persuade themselves to believe what they are saying. There are two ways liars will try
to oversell you with words and phrases. First is noncontracted denials. When people break apart a contraction, it could mean they are
emphasizing what they are saying and possibly trying to convince you
to believe them. Examples include: "I did not, I would not, I have not,
this will not," and "that cannot." Liars may try to convince us by
breaking apart contractions; truthful people usually use them. Again,
we'll look at Bill Clinton's famous *I-did-not-have-sexual-relations-
with-that-woman-Miss-Lewinsky* speech. Clinton not only used a noncontracted denial, but as he said this, he slowed his rate of speech and
pointed his finger; all indicators of someone trying to oversell their

174

lie. The second method of overselling is the use of "never" and "absolutely." If you ask a person a yes-or-no question, you should get a yes-or-no response. If you get a narrative response or a substitute for "yes" or "no," it could mean that person is trying to convince you of a lie. Since lying can be uncomfortable and most people become nervous when they lie, liars will usually avoid answering "yes-or-no" questions when it means they have to lie. To avoid committing to a firm yes or no, liars tend to replace the word "no" with "never" and "yes" with "absolutely" or "100 percent." Lance Armstrong lied to everyone about taking steroids for seven years while he was cycling and winning the Tour de France. When he was being questioned under oath (before he came clean during his Oprah interview), he answered a yes-or-no question about denying a specific conversation he had with a nurse who claimed he admitted to taking performance-enhancing drugs by saying, "Absolutely, 100 percent." The question was, "Do you deny the statements . . . uh . . . Miss Andrew attributed to you in the Indiana University State Hospital?" That is a terrible question because it is leading and confusing, but even so, it is a yes-or-no question and all Lance had to do was say, "Yes." But he doesn't. He says, "Absolutely, 100 percent," as though he is trying to convince us of his lie, which he was. While saying this, Lance was also shaking his head no! Two indicators of deception.

SOFTENING

Softening language is used by people to make an unpleasant circumstance or a violent truth less harsh than the reality. It can appear polite and nonaccusatory. However, when questioning someone and they use softening language, it could be an indicator of deception as they may be trying to cover up the harshness of what happened. It doesn't always mean someone is lying, but it can signify they are not entirely open and honest. When I would ask my litigants on *Couples Court* if they cheated on their significant others, they would tell me, "I messed around a bit." It was my job to find out what "messed around" meant. And usually, it meant sex.

You may use softening language when talking about a topic that makes you uncomfortable. For instance, if you have to fire someone from a job, you may choose to deliver that news using softer language by telling the person you have to *let them go*. Other examples are when we refer to arguing as disagreeing, fighting as horsing around, and pushing as bumping. If someone uses softening language, they do not want to confront reality.

Amanda Knox is another name most of you have probably heard. She was the roommate of Meredith Kercher while the two were living in Perugia, Italy, on a foreign exchange program. Kercher was murdered, and Knox was one of the prime suspects along with her Italian boyfriend and known burglar, Rudy Guede. At one point, Knox confessed to the Italian authorities she was in the flat when Kercher was murdered, but she recanted her statement. She was exonerated in 2015, and due to DNA evidence, Guede went to prison for killing Kercher. During an interview with Chris Cuomo in 2014, Cuomo asks Knox about the murder. At one point, Knox says, "If Rudy Guede committed this crime, which he did, we know that because his DNA is there, on the—on Meredith's body around Meredith's body, his handprints and footprints in her blood, none of that exists for me, and if I were there, I would have had traces of Meredith's broken body on me. And I would have left traces of myself around—around Meredith's corpse. And I—I am not there. And that proves my innocence." She refers to Meredith's body as a "broken body" and a "corpse." Those are examples of softening. Now, I am not saying Knox is lying, but I am saying she is softening the harshness of murder.

For those of you who are statement analysis wizards already, you may have picked up on some other indicators such as her stuttering and the use of present tense verbs. Typically, when we tell a story that happened in the past, we tell it in the past tense. If we tell a story in the present tense, that can be an indicator that that particular part of the story was made up at the present moment. McClish says, "If a person is making up a story, it is not coming up in memory so they will stumble with their words." Stories coming from memory should be clear and told in the past tense. If someone is involved in a murder, they might not be able to cope internally, and will refer to it as a death. Here are some examples of softening language used in answers.

> Q: "Where were you when she was murdered?"
> A: "I was at home when she passed."
> Q: "How many times did you stab your ex-boyfriend?"
> A: "I hit him three times before I could get away."
> Q: "Why did you threaten her?"
> A: "I warned her not to do it."

ASSUMING

This language can be tricky to correctly identify as a possible indicator of dishonesty because so many people have adopted these words or phrases as part of their everyday speech; they have become pet words, meaning they are overused. A few common sayings that can be considered assuming language are "you know," "obviously," "I already told you," and "you already know." When people say them, they expect us to take for granted that they are being honest. For example, if I asked a litigant who is denying any wrongdoing, "Are you being honest with me?" and they reply, "Obviously," that is not the same as saying, "Yes." Then, I have a problem because it is not "obvious" to me. Until he answers "yes" or states "I'm being honest," I cannot trust him. Remember back in chapter 5 when I described the NFL Deflategate scandal in which Tom Brady was accused of deflating the footballs before a game? During a press conference, a reporter asked Brady, "Is it important for you and the legacy of this team that someone is held accountable?" Brady's response is worth repeating: "Well that's for, you know I'm not the one that imposes, you know, those type of, you know accountability, it's, you know, discipline, all that, that's, you know, not really my job, so . . ." Is this assuming language or Tom's pet phrase? Unfortunately I will never know because I haven't had the chance to baseline his speech.

NONCOMMITTAL

People use noncommittal or "squishy" language when they are unsure of what they are saying; sometimes they are telling the truth, and sometimes they are covering it up. Noncommittal language can express uncertainty, intentional ambiguity, or dishonesty. Evasive individuals typically make statements using noncommittal language so that they do not have to commit to something that makes them feel uncomfortable, such as a lie. When a person tries to avoid an interviewer's questions, they will use noncommittal language. Examples include words and phrases such as "kind of," "I guess," "perhaps," "approximately," and "sort of." For example, if you asked me, "How many miles is it to the International Space Station from Earth?" my answer would be, "It is probably about three hundred miles." After all, I don't know the information. During an interview, I asked one of the litigants on *Couples Court*, "Why do you want to be with your girlfriend?" He answered, "I guess I love her." I knew the relationship was over. There is a time and a place for noncommittal language; when we don't know the information. If someone should know specific details and they use this language, they are not committing to their answer. Some people may even inflect their voice at the end of their answer as though they were asking a question instead of making a statement.

In November 2013, a shocking news story aired involving a waitress named Dayna Morales at the Gallop Asian Bistro in Bridgewater, New Jersey. Morales alleged that a family had neglected to leave her a tip and instead left her a mean note on the receipt because they didn't "approve of her lifestyle." Morales was openly gay. She photographed the receipt and posted it on her Facebook page. The photo showed a line through the tip area and a handwritten note that read, "I'm sorry, but I cannot tip because I do not agree with with your life-style." (I'll dissect this note in a minute for you; and yes, she wrote "with with." That is not a typo.) Well, her post went viral, as you can imagine, and got a lot of people upset and angry for how Danya was treated. She claimed to be a Marine Corps veteran, she was working for a living, she had to endure the disrespect and ignorance from strangers that she waited on, and then they stiffed her a tip and left a hateful message. NBC 4 New York caught wind of this story and went to the Gallop Asian Bistro to interview her. When you watch the interview, you will see that Danya doesn't get mad, she states she doesn't want to get even, but she wanted everyone to know what she endured. After seeing her on the news, anonymous people started sending her money. She collected over $3,000 from people who empathized with her and just wanted her to be treated fairly. She wasn't even keeping the money; she set up a fund to donate it to Wounded Warriors. I mean, wow, what a moral human—or so everyone thought. Everyone but me.

A week or so later, a couple who were watching this story on NBC 4 noticed it was their bill. The problem was, they had tipped her 20 percent and never wrote that message. So they contacted the TV station, which sent a reporter to interview the couple, and their interview aired. Now people were really confused. Who was telling the truth and who was lying? Morales was lying.

In the first interview, she is asked how she felt about being left that message and no tip. Her response was, "I guess I felt offended? Mad? I didn't know how to act." Let me say that if this really did happen, she would have known exactly how she felt. One of Morales's former coworkers at another restaurant prior to this event told NBC 4 that Morales came in with her head shaved one day and told coworkers she had brain cancer. But she never had brain cancer. She was also dishonorably discharged from the US Marine Corps. Morales was a con artist.

Let's look at that note again. "I'm sorry, but I cannot tip because I do not agree with with your lifestyle." First, it starts off with an "I" word and a contraction ("I'm sorry"), both indicative of truthfulness. So I believe that she is sorry for the lie she is about to tell. Then she uses the coordinating conjunction "but." This is a fickle word because we all use it often, but (see, I used it!) when we use it, it can negate what we say before it. So, in theory, the "but" in Morales's note negates "I'm sorry." Then we see her use two noncontracted denials ("I cannot . . . I do not"), which is a convincing technique, and then finally her double word, "with with." Remember what McClish says. If she is making up a story and it is not coming from her memory, she will stumble with her words. That is why you see "with with." Morales was making up this lie as she was writing it.

STORYTELLING

A story is an account of real or imaginary events. When you are listening to someone recall an event, pay attention to these words and phrases: "meanwhile," "at the time," "once," and "back then." These words could signify the story was invented: "Meanwhile" and "at that time" could be clues that the person is not speaking from memory or telling a rehearsed story, but that they are making it up as they go along or changing details as they recite it.

As humans, we have a need for knowledge. We want to make sense of everything, and when we can't, we tend to make up information that fits as the missing piece of the puzzle. In an *Atlantic Monthly* article titled, "Why Storytellers Lie," author and scholar Jonathan Gottschall writes, "The storytelling mind—the human mind, in other words—is allergic to uncertainty, randomness, and coincidence. It doesn't like to believe life is accidental; it wants to believe everything happens for a reason. Stories allow us to impose order on the chaos." Liars will use storytelling language to give their lies an order to make them more believable both to others and themselves.

In storytelling, you will also hear liars use self-talk. Self-talk refers to when a person says, "I said to myself . . ." "Where was I . . ." or "So, let me see . . ." If a person is talking out loud to themselves, they could be struggling to come up with a story. McClish says, "They are searching for information; it is not coming from their memory." Before Anthony Weiner admitted to lying about the tweet he sent, he used self-talk during an interview when he said, "I said, 'Let's try to figure out who, how, what this, how this prank went down.'"

FLUFF

Fluff, as I mentioned earlier, is the nonpertinent, random, unnecessary information people want to give me so they can avoid giving me pertinent details and answering my questions. Truthful people offer definitive responses; deceptive people sometimes pad their statements with nonpertinent information. The reason why they do this is to come across as cooperative and honest. But the reality is, they are avoiding giving you the information you are asking for.

I came up with the word "fluff" one day out of the blue when I was debriefing my class of thirty or so police officers after an exercise where they try to convince the class of a lie. I remember saying to one student, "All you gave us was fluff, so I knew you were lying." And everybody in the class looked at me funny. I went on to explain what I meant by fluff. Now everyone I have trained uses this term. I find it amusing because at the time I couldn't think of a better way to describe the nonsense I was hearing.

Fluff should not be confused with the smoke screen, which is a ruse or disguise to hide the true intentions. Liars use smoke screens to take your focus off of them and put it on something or someone else. For example, when I worked on *Couples Court* and asked the litigants why their partners accused them of cheating, they would try to smoke-screen me by saying, "My wife has no confidence in herself. She thinks

I am cheating with everyone I work with!" The smoke screen is taking my attention off of them and on to how "crazy" their partner is. People often use this technique to try to appear honest and truthful.

Fluff leaves you asking yourself, "What the heck does that have to do with anything?" When a person provides information unrelated to the matter at hand or provides information that does not answer the question asked, that person may be trying to appear cooperative by responding to your questions. But if their responses do not answer the question, or are out of context, you will have to keep searching for the truth. Sometimes people will provide irrelevant information to make themselves look naive, so you will cease asking questions. They may even be overly friendly and polite. But don't be fooled. They are most likely trying to convince you they are being cooperative and truthful when they are not. People will use fluff to conceal the truth.

UNNECESSARY WORDS

When I teach statement analysis, I use a CNN video of a former Trump University instructor, James Harris, as an example of unnecessary words. In the video he is being questioned about his claim that he was a rags-to-riches real estate guru. The interviewer confronted Harris with evidence that he was in fact a fraud. "What do you know about real estate?" the interviewer asked him. That is a good, open-ended question; it may be a bit vague, but it should have gotten a conversation going in which the interviewer could follow up with more specific questions. Instead, Harris responded by saying, "Uh . . . real estate is a very wide, huge business; um, I got involved in real estate personally myself in the '90s." That is a great example of fluff and unnecessary words. Did he answer the question? No. Did he give any pertinent information? No. This response tells me he probably doesn't know much about real estate. First, you can tell he was caught off guard because he stalls with a filler word, "uh," to buy time to think of his answer. If the answer were informative, I wouldn't mind the filler word, but what follows the filler word "uh" is fluff: "Real estate is a very wide, huge business." He hesitates again by using another filler word, "um," and goes on to say, "I got involved in real estate personally myself in the '90s." Not only was that not what he was asked, but he uses unnecessary words: "personally myself." The sentence would have made sense with either one of those words; he didn't need both. So why do people use unnecessary words? Because they don't know what to say. Anxiety is creeping in, and the brain is getting overworked.

I asked Mark McClish why liars use unnecessary words or, as Janine Driver calls it, "double talk." He said, "Extra words give you extra information. The shortest sentence is the best. If there are words that can be removed and the sentence is still grammatically correct, there is no need for extra words. The reason why liars use extra words is because they are trying to convince you of something." Harris said "personally myself" because he wanted to convince himself that he knows about real estate. He is overselling his point. McClish went on to say, "Truthful people do it with adjectives. Here is an example I use: 'I saw Bob in his blue truck.' The word 'blue' doesn't have to be there, but it gives us more information. It indicates Bob has another truck that is not blue. Deceptive people use extra words to convince you. 'I've never seen him at all.' There is no need for 'at all.'"

REPETITION

I conducted statement analysis on one of the DC Snipers for a *Profiler Task Force* episode on YouTube. If you are not familiar with the DC Snipers, there were two of them: John Allen Muhammad and his apprentice, if you will, Lee Boyd Malvo. Muhammad, who was forty-one years old at the time, and Malvo, who was seventeen, terrorized the area around Washington, DC, Northern Virginia, and Maryland back in October 2002. Over a period of about three weeks, they went on a killing spree shooting innocent civilians who were pumping gas, shopping at grocery stores, and mowing their lawns. They killed ten people during these attacks (in addition to seven they had killed in other states). There were eventually caught by the authorities. Muhammad was sentenced to death and executed on November 10, 2009. Malvo is currently serving multiple consecutive life sentences.

Here is a snippet from one of the statements Lee Boyd Malvo made while in prison: "We can never change what happened. There's nothing I can say, no apologies, there's nothing I can say, except that don't allow me and my actions to continue to victimize you for the rest of your life. It may sound cold, but it isn't. It's the only sound thing I can offer." You will notice he repeats "there's nothing I can say." Repetition of words and phrases can show sensitivity or affectation, or it can indicate that the person is being dismissive or doesn't know what else to say. It doesn't necessarily mean deception, but it can if that person is refusing to answer a question. In Malvo's statement, I find it odd that after the second time he repeats "there's nothing I can say," he has something to say: ". . . except that don't allow me and my actions to continue to victimize you for the rest of your life. It may sound cold, but it isn't." Actually, Malvo, it is cold, which makes sense because you are a cold-blooded killer. I believe Malvo repeats the phrase because he has disdain for the topic and is unwilling to give it serious attention. That may not tell you if he is lying, but it sure can tell you a lot about his demeanor and his attitude about what he did.

PASSIVE VOICE AND PRONOUNS

I am going to conclude this chapter by discussing two common and accurate indicators of deception. Do you remember Jodi Arias? She murdered her boyfriend Travis Alexander in 2008. When she was first questioned by the authorities, Jodi had a very weak cover story. She said two masked individuals broke into Travis's home while they were both there and killed him while leaving her untouched. When that story fell apart, she came up with another lie. This time she admitted to killing Travis but in self-defense. During her trial for first-degree murder, she was on the stand being cross-examined by a prosecution attorney. Here is part of the question-and-answer dialogue between her and the attorney:

> ATTORNEY: "That's when he was coming at you in this line-backer pose, right?"
> JODI: "Around that time, yes."
> ATTORNEY: "And that's when you shot him in the face, right?"
> JODI: "Um . . . ya, that's when the gun went off."

FBI deception expert Frank Marsh told Janine Driver and me, "Liars don't use proper grammar." He was right. Let's look at Jodi's grammar violations. The lawyer asked her a leading question as identified by his last inflected word, "right?" He was leading her to agree that Travis was coming at her in a linebacker pose probably because that was the story she gave previously. He knew it was bullshit, so he was trying to catch her in a lie. But instead of saying "yes" to confirm this statement, she says, "Around that time." That is not a *yes*. She says "yes" after this clause, but liars think they have to convince us of the lie, so they will usually add more information than necessary. Truthful people usually do not feel they have to convince us of the truth, so they have no problem answering a yes-or-no question with a simple yes or no. Had Jodi Arias been telling the truth, she would have simply answered, "Yes." Her deceptive response (intended to convince, not to convey) tells me Travis probably didn't come at her in a linebacker pose.

Next, the lawyer asks another leading question: "And that's when you shot him in the face, right?" Jodi violates the rules of grammar by responding with, "Um . . . ya, that's when the gun went off." First, she stalls by using a filler word, "um." Then she uses the passive voice instead of the active voice, which is common when people lie. She says, ". . . that's when the gun went off." Okay, first, guns can't go off by themselves; someone has to pull the trigger. So that statement is a lie. And the fact that she said the gun went off (passive voice) instead of, "I fired the gun" (active voice), is a common indicator of deception and a common violation of grammar.

Here is another example I use in my classes when I teach statement analysis. This excerpt comes from a real-world witness statement. Read it and try to identify any grammar violations that indicate deception.

I picked up the gun to clean it. Moved it to the left hand to get the cleaning rod. Something bumped the trigger. The gun went off, hitting my wife.

Just like Jodi Arias, this guy used a passive voice when he stated that "the gun went off . . ." Let me walk you through a few common indicators of deception in these four sentences. First, you can see he started it off by using the personal pronoun "I." The pronouns "I" and "my" show accountability, responsibility, and ownership of what the person is saying. So when the husband uses "I" in this first sentence, "I picked up the gun," that tells me he is taking ownership of picking up the gun, but he doesn't take ownership of the gun. The fact that he said "the gun" and not "my gun" leaves me wondering whose gun is it? And if it was his (which it was), he should have said, "I picked up my gun to clean it." He didn't say that because he had used his gun to purposely kill his wife. Knowing that he killed his wife with intention, the gun becomes a source of guilt. He doesn't want to claim it because he doesn't want to be associated with the crime. In the second sentence, "Moved it to the left hand to get the cleaning rod," you may have caught on that again— he avoids ownership of the verb "move" and of his own left hand. He writes, "the left hand." He should have said "my left hand." You now know there is a reason why he didn't: to avoid guilty ownership of the crime. I bet he didn't realize that he replaced "my" with "the." Most liars have no idea of what they are or aren't saying. Remember, most liars focus on controlling their body language, not their spoken language. Liars avoid "I" and "my" unwittingly, so be sure to listen carefully when people speak. You should have noticed one more thing wrong with this sentence: he started it off without an "I." He started with the verb: "Moved it to the left hand." Another example of a lack of accountability for what he is telling us. There is a reason why people leave out the "I." It is done unconsciously, but not accidentally.

Let's look at the third sentence: "Something bumped the trigger." The word "bumped" is softening language. Triggers do not get bumped, they get pulled. He also states that *something* bumped it. Now, if this gun is in his left hand, how would he not know what bumped the trigger? It was his index finger!

And finally, in the last sentence, "The gun went off, hitting my wife," he uses classic liar's language: passive voice. You probably noticed he did take accountability of his wife, however. In total there are six indicators that this is a lie, and it was. This guy shot and killed his wife and was later convicted of first-degree murder.

Active voice emphasizes the subject doing an action, and passive voice emphasizes that the subject received the action. Liars tend to use passive voice to distance themselves from a crime or the event with which they have a guilty association. Passive voice allows them to leave out the subject, which is usually them, and conceal their responsibility.

Another way to reduce self-references is to substitute the personal pronouns "I" and "my" with another pronoun such as "you," "they," "them," and "us." I'll use another infamous case of a politician who lied about a certain tweet of his private parts: yes, Anthony Weiner. Before he finally realized he was caught with his pants down, literally, he lied and denied accusations about tweeting a "dick pic" to a twenty-one-year-old woman. He was interviewed and took part in press conferences with reporters asking him point-blank yes-or-no questions such as, "Did you send the tweet?" Anthony never replied "yes" or "no," which is another accurate indicator that a person is not being truthful. When asked yes-or-no questions, as long as they aren't leading questions, honest people have no issue committing to a yes-or-no response. Some reporters called him out and actually said to him, "Anthony, all you have to do is say no!" But he never said "no." And the more they pressed him, the more belligerent he became, eventually losing his composure. He was in defensive mode. As you know by now, you don't want to back a person into a corner when you have confronted them in a lie. You have to adopt a non-accusatory approach and create a safe environment to give you an honest answer. In Weiner's case, that would be a "yes."

Here are some more examples of passive voice:

- "The safe was left unlocked" rather than "I left the safe unlocked."
- "The shipment was authorized" rather than "I authorized the shipment."

When I conduct statement analysis, I pay particular attention to the passive voice and the presence or absence of personal pronouns. First-person singular pronouns are important, as you saw in the examples at the beginning of this chapter with Jodi Arias and the murderous husband. The personal pronoun "I" (including "I'm," "I'll," "I'd," "I've," and related contractions) is an accurate indication that a person is being honest—unless it is overused. Liars who are trying to convince you of a lie may overuse "I" statements. Because most liars experience cognitive overload when pressed for details, their ability to formulate complex sentences decreases and what you end up hearing are short "I" statements.

If someone hesitates to use "I" and they replace it with another pronoun such as "you" or "we," there is a reason why. They do not

188

want to take accountability for what they are saying or be associated with the event they are describing. I have already used Anthony Weiner as an example, but because he is such an excellent case study for deceptive indicators, here is another one. Before he admitted to sexting his private parts, he told a news reporter, "Look, we're trying to figure out who did this." Can you hear the problem? He replaced "I" with "we." You all now know there was no "we" because he knew all along he was the perpetrator. He should have said, "I'm trying to figure out who sent this tweet from my Twitter account," but he didn't want to be associated with a lie.

• • •

"The most important thing in communication is to hear what isn't being said."

—PETER DRUCKER

ACTIVITY

This is a fun activity. Ask a friend, colleague, or someone you know well to handwrite a story that is a complete lie. Tell this person to create a believable lie (so they should not write about having supernatural powers). The story only has to be the length of one side of an 8 x 11 sheet of paper. The reason why you want this person to handwrite their story and not type it is because, if they type it, they can go back and make changes to what they have written. We do not want them to do that because we want to be able to see the lies. After they finish, you will conduct statement analysis on their story to see if they can identify any of the verbal indicators of deception covered in this chapter. Have fun, but please do not do this exercise on your husband or wife!

EPILOGUE

WANTED TO WRAP up this book by leaving you with some final thoughts. Communication is an art and a science. In fact, my company's byline is, "Where the art & science of human interaction meet." The interviewer and interviewee ebb and flow in their words and behaviors because they play off each other and influence each other's behaviors. The interviewer is influenced by the interviewee regarding which techniques to use; the interviewee is influenced by the interviewer on whether or not to be open and honest.

Interviewing and negotiating are mental sparring games. You must know *what* to say, *when* to say it, and *how* to say it. That comes with practice and being self- and situationally aware. Self-awareness allows us to look at ourselves from the outside. Situational awareness allows us to look at others through an objective lens. Without this awareness, we will not be able to relate to others in such a way that we can persuade them to be open and honest with us.

Awareness allows us to pick up on verbal and nonverbal subtleties, so we know how to keep the stress level down and rapport level up. You have to be flexible and patient with yourself and others and trust in your ability to use the techniques I have provided for you. If you can do that, you will master any interview or conversation you want.

I know you will find uses for the information in this book in your life. My motto is always to remain a student, a seeker of knowledge. My duty is to share the knowledge I have with others to help them achieve success. I hope I was able to do that for you. Please contact me at lenasisco@thecongruencygroup.com to inquire about my training and consulting services.

• • •

"Unaware, we will project our intentions on their behavior and call ourselves objective."

—STEPHEN COVEY

APPENDIX A

11-STEP STRATEGIC INTERVIEW FLOW

HAVE BEEN ASKED numerous times what my "flow" is when I am interrogating/interviewing. I never realized I had one until I started thinking strategically about my interviewing method. The interview flow follows the conversational hourglass. You have to ease into and out of the interview, always focusing on rapport and creating a safe environment so POIs feel comfortable being honest.

At the midpoint of the hourglass/interview, after you have gained the POI's trust, you have to do the dance. The POI will be forthcoming, then resist; they may open back up, then shut down. It's like ocean waves lapping at the shore. You have to flow with their demeanor and behavior. That's why I call it my "interview flow." During Step 5 you may have to go back to Step 2; during Step 9 you may have to go back to Step 4.

Here are eleven steps to my "flow":

1. Get their interest immediately.
2. Gain their trust through rapport.
3. Carefully control the conversation to the topic of concern.
4. Do the dance:

Ask direct and indirect questions.
Use questioning techniques.

Reinforce the rapport.

Exploit all information.

Identify indicators of truthfulness and deception/conduct statement analysis.

Gently push them to cognitive overload.

5. Call out the elephant in the room (tell them you know they are lying).
6. Bring them to the breaking point by causing cognitive overload.
7. Assign a positive trait.
8. Be patient, listen, be empathetic, know when to push and when to ease up.
9. After they break, exploit all details.
10. Reinforce rapport, leave them feeling positive and open to speaking with you again.
11. Establish recontact procedures.

YOUR COMPREHENSIVE INTERVIEW CHECKLIST

CHAPTER 2: PLAN, PREP, AND PRACTICE

Before you interview, fill in the following:

- Objective(s):
- Time:
- Location:
- Strategic focus:
- POI information (as detailed as you can to include behavior and demeanor):
- Note-taking:
- Recording (audio/video):
- Interviewers:
- Interpreters:
- Room setup:
- Create a list of the "what-ifs":

CHAPTER 3: HOW TO BUILD RAPPORT IN FIVE MINUTES OR LESS

Before you interview, think of how you will build rapport with your POI:

- What do you have in common? How can you connect with them within the first five minutes? Exploit the similar-to-me bias.
- How will you mirror their behaviors?
- How will you change your language so you are not accusatory and do not tell them what they *can't* do?
- What positive trait can you assign this person?
- Be a team, not an opponent.
- Change the scene if necessary.
- Find out everything you can about the person you are interviewing.

CHAPTER 4: UNDERSTANDING PERSONAL DRIVERS, MOTIVATORS, AND NEEDS

Before you interview, answer the following questions:

- Is your POI inward or outward focused?
- How can you use the laddering technique?
- What is their motivation to tell the truth? What needs will you have to meet for them to tell the truth?

CHAPTERS 5, 6 & 7: MASTER YOUR QUESTIONING TECHNIQUES; DON'T TELL, ASK; AND ELICIT INFORMATION, DON'T ASK FOR IT

Before you interview, plan your questions:

- Write out specific questions you will ask.
- Write out any yes-or-no questions you will ask only to check for truthfulness.
- What repeat and control interrogatives will you ask?
- Remember to fully exploit a topic by asking follow-up interrogatives.

- Do not ask leading, forced choice, vague, compound, loaded, or negative questions.
- Do not tell someone what they did or why they did it; ask interrogatives instead: What did you do? Why did you do it?
- Use elicitation (indirect questioning) when questioning has created an uncomfortable environment. Ease any stress and relax the POI by switching to using elicitation techniques to extract pertinent information.
- How can you use the five questioning techniques to help you get the truth?
    1. Which non-pertinent questions can you ask to relax the POI?
    2. Adopt a pause to make sure you give the POI time to answer.
    3. When can you exploit a topic by using rapid fire to increase cognitive overload?
    4. Use the Columbo Approach.
    5. Timeline their story.
- Use my four lie-exposing questions:
    1. How did that make you feel?
    2. Why should I believe you?
    3. What do you think should happen to the person who ...?
    4. Are you a liar? Did you lie to me?

CHAPTER 9: EMPATHIC NEGOTIATION SKILLS

Profile your target:

- What is your NPT? (HE-e, HE-i, HI-e, HI-i, SE-e, SE-i, SI-e, SI-i)

Plan your approach to an empathic negotiation:

- Do it in person, face-to-face.
- Put yourself in the other person's shoes.
- Build rapport.
- Come prepared with facts and data.
- Be prepared to say no.
- Use empathetic statements to create a safe environment.
- Use elicitation techniques to encourage your opponent to open up.
- Don't be afraid to show vulnerability.
- Use a confident voice.
- Check in with your biases.
- Do not try to pretend to be something you are not.

Plan your conversation:

- What is your objective?
- What is your BOND?
- What is their WHY?

CHAPTER 10: HANDLING THE BREAKING POINT

To effectively handle the breaking point so that the POI breaks instead of shuts down, you need to figure out what will motivate them to confess. The breaking point can come when the POI knows you have discovered their lie. We want to let the POI know we know they lied without being accusatory. To do this, you can say the following:
"It appears to me . . ."

- ". . . that there is something else you want to tell me." (Avoid saying, "there is something else you are not telling me," because that may be accusatory and cause them to shut down.)
- ". . . that there is more to the story."
- ". . . that there is something else on your mind."

You can also say, "I may be wrong, but . . ."

- ". . . I sense some hesitation in your answers."
- ". . . you appear to be uncomfortable." (You can ask a follow-on question after they answer, such as, "What can I do to gain your trust?" or, "What can I do to make you feel comfortable?")

You can also persuade them to break by using embedded commands. You can say, "I notice that when I questioned you about [insert topic] . . ."

- ". . . you became nervous."
- ". . . you looked like you felt guilt."
- ". . . you looked like you wanted to tell me something."

You can say, "Now that you know I have discovered discrepancies in your story . . ."

- ". . . you are feeling guilty."
- ". . . you want to come clean."

You can say, "Eventually . . ."

- ". . . you will tell me the truth because it is the right thing to do."
- ". . . the burden of lying will break your will."
- ". . . you will accept I caught you in a lie—we have evidence that points to you."

You can also say:

- "It's not easy to lie; you will get confused."

- "No one can remember a rehearsed story; you will forget the details."
- "You may notice how worried you feel right now."
- "You are probably starting to think that telling me that lie was a bad idea."
- "You are probably starting to think it's time to come clean and tell me the truth."
- "Remember, everyone leaks indicators of deception, and I am trained to pick up on them."
- "Tell me why I don't believe you."

The POI needs to feel good about themselves and finally do the right thing.

APPENDIX C

ANSWERS TO ACTIVITIES

CHAPTER 3: HOW TO BUILD RAPPORT IN FIVE MINUTES OR LESS

Activity: Change negative language to positive.

- "You're being rude." Change that to nonaccusatory language and say, "There seems to be a lack of politeness."
- "You can't treat me like that." Change that to positive language and say, "You will treat me with respect."
- "You're going to miss the deadline." Change that to nonaccusatory language and ask, "Do you think you will make the deadline?"
- "You aren't leaving until I have that report." Change that to positive language and say, "You can leave as soon as I have that report."
- "You never hear anything I say." Change that to positive language and say, "You will hear what I have to say," or, "Thank you for listening and hearing everything I say."
- "You could care less about what I think." Change that to nonaccusatory language and say, "I know you care about what I think."
- "Don't tell me that you've changed." Change that to positive language and say, "Tell me how you have changed."

- "Don't raise your voice to me." Change that to non-accusatory language and say, "Let's talk without raising our voices."
- "You misinterpreted what I said." Change that to nonaccusatory language and say, "Perhaps what I said wasn't clear."
- "Why are you so angry?" Change that to non-accusatory language and say, "How do you feel right now?"

CHAPTER 4: UNDERSTANDING PERSONAL DRIVERS, MOTIVATORS, AND NEEDS

Activity: Laddering

In the following three scenarios, come up with at least five probing questions you would ask to find out the POI's motivations to tell the truth. There are no right or wrong answers. Just be sure to begin the question with "why" or "how."

Scenario 1: POI is a seventeen-year-old girl who is being interviewed by her principal about marijuana that fell out of her bag during class. The girl's mother is sitting beside her. The girl claims she has no idea how the marijuana got in her bag. You think she is lying. What probing questions could you ask her? Your objective is to find out her motivation and need in order to get her to tell the truth.

- How do you feel about the fact that the teacher saw the marijuana fall out of your bag?
- How do you feel about teenagers using marijuana?
- Why do you believe teenagers in this school smoke marijuana?
- How do you feel about marijuana?
- Why would anyone hide the fact that they are smoking marijuana?

Scenario 2: You are an executive recruiter, and your potential job candidate will not answer your calls or return them. It has been one week since they said they were going to talk to their boss about terminating their employment so that you can place them in your client's company. They finally answer your call and apologize for not being able to call you back because they got busy, and they were sick, and their car died. You don't believe them. What probing questions can you ask to find out why they are ghosting you? Your objective is to find out their motivation and need in order to get them to terminate their job and join the new company.

- How do you feel about our communication over this past week?
- Why do you think we haven't spoken since last week?
- How do you feel about your new opportunity/job?
- Why do you think this new opportunity is a good change for you?
- Why would you feel you should take this new job?

Scenario 3: As an entrepreneur, your goal this year is to grow your clients and your income significantly. You have been networking and marketing your program on social media. A potential client contacts you and wants to know how much you charge for one-on-one coaching services. You tell them your price. They scoff and try to negotiate your price with you, which is nonnegotiable. What probing questions can you ask this person to find out why they do not want to pay your asking price? Your objective is to have this person be excited to pay your asking price and become your new client.

- Why do you feel the price is not fair?
- Why would you want to negotiate the price?
- How do you determine the fairness of prices?
- Why do you feel the price is negotiable?

- How would you handle negotiating something that is nonnegotiable?

202

CHAPTER 5: MASTER YOUR QUESTIONING TECHNIQUES

Activity A: Change ineffective questions to effective questions.

- "Are you mad?" to "How do you feel right now?"
- "Do you take the bus or drive to work in the morning?" to "How do you get to work in the morning?"
- "Will you be arriving early?" to "When you will be arriving?"
- "Won't you ever stop complaining?" to "When will you stop complaining?" / "Why are you complaining?" / "What are you complaining about?"
- "Do you prefer your mother's cooking or your grand-mother's?" to "Whose cooking do you prefer in your family?"
- "Were they upset with what happened?" to "How did they feel about what happened?"
- "Didn't you say she said 'no' when you asked her?" to "What did she say when you asked her?"
- "Is she applying for jobs?" to "What jobs did she apply for?"

Activity B: Ten effective, specific interrogative questions you can ask an author within two minutes.

1. How long did it take you to write your book?
2. How did you come up with the topic of your book?
3. What inspired you to write your book?
4. Who is your publishing agent?
5. How much money will you make from this publication?
6. What is the name of the publishing company that published your book?

7. Where can someone purchase your book?
8. When will your book be available to purchase?
9. When will your write another book?
10. How difficult was it to write your book?

CHAPTER 6: DON'T TELL, ASK

Activity: Here are three scenarios in chapter 6, with an alternative "Don't Tell, Ask" question/statement to replace the minimizing-the-event statement.

Scenario #1: Coworker Clash

Good Morning, Rodney! As the new COO, I am excited to work together to make this company successful. In order to do that, I need your help. Even though we are all very busy at this time, as your senior supervisor, I would appreciate your time for a fifteen-minute meeting this week. I would like you to brief me on your position so I can learn more about your role and initiatives and so we can work together as an effective team. I value your openness and honest communication with me. Thank you. Sincerely, Alicia.

Scenario #2: Tight-Lipped Witness

You are a detective interviewing a witness to a neighborhood crime. You say, "If you don't tell us what you saw, these people will continue to vandalize the neighborhood, or worse, hurt people. How do you feel about that?" Wait for an answer and continue to exploit.

Scenario #3: Addicted Patient

"You should not be experiencing pain this long after the surgery. Percocet can be addictive and very dangerous to your organs if taken over long periods of time. I suggest you stop taking the Percocet for a week and we'll see how you feel after that. How do you feel about that?" Wait for an answer and continue to exploit.

CHAPTER 7: ELICIT INFORMATION, DON'T ASK FOR IT

Here are the suggested responses. There are no right answers, however. You may come up with more techniques to use and thus different provocative statements.

"Where do you come from?"

- "You definitely don't drive/talk like you are from around here." (Naivete)

"Where do you work?"

- "You must have an interesting occupation based on what you know about X." (Showing Interest)

"What do you think about teenagers' obsession with taking selfies?"

- "I need a teenager to help me understand why they take so many selfies." (Naivete)

"Do you play sports?"

- "You look athletic/in shape; you must play a sport." (Flattery)

"What do you like to do for fun?"

- "When I finally get some free time, and I want to have fun, I go dancing!" (Quid Pro Quo)

"What is your favorite song?"

- "Every morning I start out listening to my favorite song."
  (Quid Pro Quo)

"What is your method to flipping houses and selling at such a high profit?"

- "You must have a method you use to be able to make such a high profit." (Assumed Knowledge)

"Why do you always have to have the last word in every conversation?"

- "Having to say the last word is an ineffective communication habit. Most of us may not even realize we do it." (Criticize)

"Why did you not tell the truth when you had the chance?"

- "You had the chance to tell the truth. I can't understand why you would not want to be honest." (Express Disbelief)

"What is your nickname?"

- "I bet they called you 'Roadrunner' in high school because you were a track star." (False Statement)

"There have been four Tesla crashes in the past two months. What is wrong with them?"

- "There has got to be something wrong with manufacturing parts on the Tesla to cause all these recent crashes." (Criticize)

CHAPTER 8: OVERCOME CONVERSATIONAL CHALLENGES

Challenge Scenario Solution:

As Bob's program manager, you are meeting with Matt to give him feedback about his statement regarding wearing a COVID mask.

- "Matt, we are all frustrated with the changing rules. I'd like to hear more about your thoughts and opinions." Listen to Matt and let him vent in a safe environment. Then say:
- "Matt, I respect your point of view. And I agree with you; I am frustrated as well. But being frustrated is not a solution and will only lead to more unproductive behaviors. Let's figure out a way to deal with changing policies so that we don't react to them with anger and frustration." Follow up with:
- "Bob and I are open to hearing your thoughts anytime. We are a team so let's handle these challenges together and help each other through these difficult times. What else can I do for you right now?"

CHAPTER 11: HOW TO ACCURATELY ANALYZE BODY LANGUAGE

Chris Watts Deceptive Analysis Answers:

Throughout this interview, Watts is breathy, meaning it sounds like he is struggling for air. This happens when you are under extreme amounts of stress. His mouth is drying out from cortisol evident by licking lips and hard swallows. Watts is stressed from lying. Watts displays numerous incongruent shoulder shrugs and shakes his head "no" repeatedly. Let's discuss his incongruent facial expressions of emotion.

You should have seen the following facial expressions of emotions that are incongruent with what he is saying:

1. Contempt :44
2. Doubt :54
3. Disgust 1:12
4. Contempt 1:24

You should have also seen the following indicators of stress and deception:

- Prolonged Eyeblink :17
- Tongue Protrusion :34
- Prolonged Eyeblink :44
- Deep Inhale :51
- Prolonged Eyeblink 1:11
- Tongue Protrusion 1:22
- Prolonged Eyeblink 1:23
- Prolonged Eyeblink and Hard Swallow 1:28
- Rapid Eye Blinking 1:33
- Licking Lips 1:34
- Lips Disappear 1:35

Additional Info from 1:35 to 1:57. Here are deceptive indicators:

- At minute 1:39, he says, "I called her three times … texted her about three times" as he shrugs his shoulders and shakes his head "no." Also, he used the liar's number, three. When liars have to quantify information and they have to make it up on the spot, they usually will say three: three times, three hours, three miles, and so on. It is no coincidence Chris Watts says he called and texted her three times. He's lying.
- At minute 1:43, he stutters (cognitive overload) and shakes his head "no."
- At minute 1:46, he looks to the right and shrugs his shoulders.
- At minute 1:47, he is smiling.
- At minute 1:50, he swipes his face—itchy from stress.

ACKNOWLEDGMENTS

WANT TO EXPRESS my gratitude to everyone who helped me get past the "two-book hump." I admit I was almost satisfied at two.

My *why* for what I do and who I have become is to provide knowledge to help people make more informed decisions to protect themselves in any situation. Whether it is making a financial investment, investigating a crime, or entering into a new relationship, I have tools to help you, and it is my duty to share them with you. I want to acknowledge and thank all those who made that possible. Your effort, friendship, and support mean so much to me.

I want to express my gratitude to my family first because they are with me through it all. Thank you, Eli, for allowing me to work odd hours, such as during our nine-hour drives to Rhode Island. Second, I want to thank my agent, Maryann Karinch, for sticking with me and supporting me! Without you, Maryann, I wouldn't be here—again!

Thank you, HarperCollins and Neuwirth & Associates, Inc., for allowing me to publish my passion. I want to point out a few individuals at HarperCollins, especially Sara Kendrick and Linda Alila. You were all absolutely fantastic to work with! Thank you also to Jeff Farr, Beth Metrick, and Noah Perkins for the hard work.

And a special thank-you goes to Louis Greenstein; you had your work cut out! *Thank you* so much for polishing up my words!

And I want to give my heartfelt gratitude to Janine Driver. Your positive energy, larger-than-life personality, and immense generosity and compassion make me feel honored to be in your inner circle. *Thank you* for taking the time—while you were sick with COVID—to write the foreword. I am forever grateful.

Mark McClish, thank you so much for allowing me to interview you and share your wisdom.

Thank you to all of my friends, who have inspired me. I want to mention a few by name: Judit, I cherish our Thursday dinner discussions that led me on a new journey I am so thankful for; Toni, for your enthusiasm to help others and share your cultural knowledge; Elly, I am thrilled to be collaborating and creating the Truth Sisters Academy with you, and we have big things coming this year; Susan, you are amazing, and I have learned so much from you; Lauren, my SW, thank you for your light; Ali, you have a gift—your power of positive thought work is enlightening; your words are wisdom.

I also want to express deep gratitude to all of you who serve in law enforcement, fire and rescue, medical capacities, and the military. Thank you all for your service and your courage and commitment to keeping this world safe.

Many thanks to all of you who are reading this. It's because of you all that I can keep sharing my knowledge.

With respect,
Lena

INDEX

ABOUT THE AUTHOR

LENA SISCO is a former naval intelligence officer and Marine Corps–certified interrogator who served in the Global War on Terror conducting hundreds of interrogations. She is a published author, keynote speaker, and former TEDx speaker, and was an expert witness on an Emmy-nominated court TV show for three years. She keynotes around the world and is a speaker for SPYEX and the SPY Museum in Washington, DC.

Since 2003, Lena has been training the Department of Defense, government agencies, law enforcement, special forces, and private sector industries in interviewing and interrogation, statement analysis, body language, detecting deception, elicitation, and change leadership.

Lena is also certified in Organizational Change Management and received a certificate in the Psychology of Leadership from Cornell University. She has a master's from Brown University in archaeology, and her BA is in anthropology from the University of Rhode Island.

In 2013, Lena started her own company, The Congruency Group. You can reach her at:

lenasisco@thecongruencygroup.com

+1 703.898.6364

www.thecongruencygroup.com.